CHILD SEXUAL ABUSE: WHOSE PROBLEM?

REFLECTIONS FROM CLEVELAND

Sue Richardson and Heather Bacon (Editors), Hilary Cashman,
Marjorie Dunn, Marietta Higgs, Annette Lamballe-Armstrong,
Geoffrey Wyatt

VENTURE PRESS

Published by
VENTURE PRESS
16 Kent Street
Birmingham
B5 6RD
Tel: 021 622 3911

First Published 1991

Printed and bound in Great Britain by
Dotesios Ltd, Trowbridge, Wiltshire.

British Library Cataloguing in Publication Data

Child Sexual Abuse: Whose Problem?
I. Richardson, Sue.   II. Bacon, Heather
III. Cashman, Hilary
362.7044

ISBN 0 900 102 934 (paperback)

To the children of Cleveland from whom we
have learned so much.

Acknowledgements

We gratefully acknowledge the help of Val Hall, Karen Henderson, Tom Richardson and Louise Wynn with the preparation of the text.

Contents

Contents

Introduction: Reflections From Cleveland

Our great advantage is that we are mounted on the horse of history. And this horse can only march in one direction — forward. Sometimes it gets tired. At other times it veers slightly off track. But it never takes a step backward. The enemy, on the other hand, has the great disadvantage of marching against the current. (Tomas Borge, 1987)

It is no accident that we have chosen an analogy from a political struggle to introduce this evaluation of the dilemmas facing abused children and their advocates. The achievement of societal awareness and recognition of child sexual abuse is akin to war. We expect to see fluctuations in the balance of forces but a steady historical advance. The key to the survival of those in the forefront of the struggle is to maintain hope in the reality of this forward movement. Maintaining this optimism is arduous. We can be strengthened by sharing and evaluating our experiences with others in a climate of openness.

As professionals in Cleveland, we did not often find such a climate to be available. Child sexual abuse is a problem which depends on silence and secrecy. We have experienced something of what happens to abused children when they attempt to speak: we have been disbelieved, rejected and silenced. This book is a breaking of that silence, a return to health and an invitation to open debate. It is not a replay of the 'Cleveland Crisis' but aims to set the record straight on myths which have influenced post-Cleveland practice. We explore controversial issues regarding diagnosis, intervention and treatment from our direct involvement in the events of 1987 which were reviewed by the Butler–Sloss Inquiry.

Introduction: Reflections From Cleveland

A significant feature of our experience is that, due to developments in medical diagnosis, children were identified as allegedly abused at a pre-disclosure stage. Some of these children were very young and depended on an adult to have the courage and conviction to act as their advocate. We are proud to have acted in this capacity. However, we recognize the limitations in practice, procedures and knowledge which existed at that time. We see our subsequent learning and experience, not as the tragedy that it has been popularly depicted, but as a precious gift of knowledge which marks a new phase of awareness and development. This fact is masked in the many references to Cleveland which have been made in other texts, without benefit of access to the essential data of case material. The post-Cleveland analysis of the process of case management and inter-disciplinary conflict has therefore been divorced from content. Because of our professional isolation and (or) silencing by our legal advisers and employers, these two essential aspects of a full understanding have not previously been brought together.

Unlike child abuse itself, open discussion of the problem is a relatively new phenomenon. Because the existence of abuse has been concealed or denied for so long, the way in which professionals and families should respond has never been fully debated by the whole community. One of the reasons why it is necessary to bring all the community's resources to bear on deciding how the problem should be managed, is the high level of dissension it creates and the need to approach that conflict creatively. Cleveland is neither new nor unusual. The very first page of the Butler-Sloss Report states that what the Inquiry had thought was a local difficulty was soon seen to be part of wider problems which were not unique to Cleveland. What is unique to Cleveland, in the United Kingdom, is the emergence of informed, responsible community debate, committed to supporting the professionals under siege. We have therefore included a chapter by non-professionals on the community perspective. It is not possible for professionals to address this problem alone. Alliances are needed which aim for radical change in the way both children and their advocates are viewed and valued.

It is our hope that, by demonstrating the survival of our commitment to children despite our public, private and professional hurts, this book may be inspirational to those who are working at the frontiers or who feel demoralised or overwhelmed. For us, our experience represents a priceless clearing of the fog which surrounds child sexual abuse. We have gained in our understanding and acceptance of the tasks for child advocates and in the strengthening of our commitment to open debate about the dilemmas presented by child sexual abuse for practitioners, families and society.

Sue Richardson and Heather Bacon
December 1990

1 From Colwell to Cleveland 1973 to 1988

Marjorie Dunn

Each brief clearing of the fog brings out believers who claim fantastic insights, only to be scorned and forced to recant by those who insist that the believers have been bedazzled by an apparition, something false and dangerous. (Summit 1988)

Introduction

The first page of the report into child abuse in Cleveland in 1987 (Butler-Sloss. 1988. P.1) acknowledges how the judge and her assessors 'became increasingly aware of the large number of issues causing continuing difficulties which were not unique to Cleveland'. This chapter aims to put events in Cleveland into a wider context based on my experience as a senior nursing officer responsible for child protection in Cleveland up to and including the inquiry. It explores the local background to the working relationships and growing concern regarding child sexual abuse. A perspective is provided from which to challenge the isolation of Cleveland in response to the diagnosis, between February and July 1987, of 121 children as allegedly sexually abused .

Before we can begin to understand the conflict of Cleveland in 1987, we must look more generally at the relative position and progress of agencies involved in care and protection of children, not forgetting the parents or relatives, or those involved in the voluntary sector. We can relate the wider issues to Kempe's idea that society must go through six stages before child abuse can be eliminated. Firstly, denial that either physical or sexual abuse exists to a significant extent. Secondly, the community pays attention to the more lurid forms of abuse, such as the battered child,and begins to find ways of preventing and coping more effectively with this.

...ly, physical abuse is better managed and attention is paid to more ...le forms of abuse such as poisoning and the infant who fails to thrive. In stage four, the community recognises emotional abuse and deprivation and patterns of severe rejection. In stage five, the community acknowledges the existence of the sexually abused child. Finally, in stage six the community guarantees that each child is truly wanted and provided with loving care, decent shelter and food and first class preventive and curative health care. (Kempe and Kempe, 1978).

The World Health Organisation's document (1986) states that 'a well motivated and actively participating community is essential to the attainment of the common goal (i.e health)'. This complements the ethos of Kempe's stage six. This value base is the foundation for a child health perspective, focusing on the promotion of all aspects of health, prevention of ill health and the early identification of handicap, illness and child abuse. Even physical abuse was not widely recognised until the publication of a paper in 1962 by Kempe, entitled 'The Battered Child Syndrome'. The use of the emotive term 'battered babies' aroused interest and concern in professionals and public. It is fascinating to consider the development of community acceptance of physical abuse and maltreatment of children and relate it to the stages reached in awareness and acknowledgement of sexual abuse.

The stages that society has to move through to recognise child sexual abuse, (Kempe and Kempe, 1978) will inevitably generate conflict. This must be recognised as an essential part of the process and a mechanism established to deal with it, resulting in the development of a common belief system. This can help us to understand how the Cleveland crisis came about, in that different sections of the community – professionals, parents, agencies – were at different stages.

Cleveland : Historical Perspective

Increased awareness of child physical abuse has led to public outcry and inquiry when children die. Marie Colwell was returned to her mother and step-father by social services after several years in a foster family. She became the family drudge and scapegoat, but bruising and cruel treatment were not reported by shopkeepers, school teachers, neighbours and others until after she was killed by her step-father (Colwell, 1974). Somehow the concerns were not communicated to or acknowledged by those who had the power to protect her. Professionals involved were blamed for Maria's death. Effectively, this has happened each time a child has died at the hands of an adult care giver.

The events surrounding the child sexual abuse crisis in Cleveland created horror and controversy, this time because a number of children were removed from their homes on suspicion of being sexually abused. However, in this case the controversy, which involved both the public and professionals, settled around the belief that children who had not been sexually abused were abused by being removed from their families.

1987 was not the first time that an 'outbreak' of public awareness about child abuse had occurred in Cleveland. Ferguson (1989 and 1990) traced the antecedents, using NSPCC records. During an initial 'rescue' period, from the end of the 19th century to the end of the second world war, the NSPCC started working in Cleveland. In 1892 they provided 'shelters' in Middlesborough and Stockton which they called 'places of safety'. Children were described as having their lips permanently sealed unless they were in safe surroundings. Although the 'place of safety' was to meet that need, some children still could not disclose their abuse and were returned home very quickly without prosecution of an abuser. Attempts were largely made to protect children by removing 'bad' parents from the home, the key phrase being 'enforcing of parental responsibility'. Incarceration was to reform them into useful citizens. The resulting duties laid down de-emphasised the role of disclosure work with children and heightened the community's resistance to intervention. Self-initiated referrals by NSPCC Inspectors then dropped rapidly from twenty-seven percent to two percent. In 1904 public concern led to a visit from the NSPCC Director to Cleveland to reassure the public that 'NSPCC inspectors did not hang around street corners looking for cases'. In 1908 legal and social policies were formally enacted and the punishment of incest became part of criminal law, but the terms were so tightly constrained that less than two percent of cases fell within the act. By 1914 thirty-five percent of cases were being referred by child-care professionals. A case history from 1909 makes familiar reading. Emily was an 11 year old from a family of four children cared for by their father. Their mother was dead. There was a history of poor and neglectful parenting. The children were described as dirty but not 'failing to thrive'. When Emily was interviewed she said 'I don't like sleeping with him because he hurts me in bed. It makes him bad in the morning and me too – gives me stomach ache. He used to do it to my sister and started to do it to me when she left'. Medical examination found that there was genital soreness and the hymen was absent but the opinion was that this was not consistent with penetration. Therefore the medical evidence could not be used to confirm Emily's story. Neglect charges were substantiated and the father received a two-month prison sentence. The Director of Public Prosecutions did not press other charges and Emily was taken into care by the NSPCC. Children had to overcome resistance to disclosure by themselves: Emily invited state intervention by asking her sister to go to the NSPCC. Public ambivalence to child abuse was strong: child abusers were portrayed in the press as shocking, disgusting and fascinating. These aspects of increased awareness of child abuse also characterised the events of 1987, but with one difference : the orchestration of public response in 1987. (Ferguson, 1989).

Developing Awareness

Society relies on the media reporting of child abuse as the source of its knowledge and beliefs. Since this is usually of a sensational nature, opinions tend to be negative, punitive and denying. Professionals however have widely varying opportunities to learn, depending on their job, the area they are employed in, the availability of training opportunities, and not least, their own interest and commitment. The reluctance of some front-line professionals to acknowledge incidents of abuse, and societal denial of all but the most media-catching horrors, create major difficulties in intervening. It is preferable to see people who hurt their children as monsters, sick, wicked, and far removed from one's acquaintances or relatives. In Cleveland, as elsewhere, professionals with some understanding of the multi-factorial reasons contributing to the pathology of abuse were seen as over-sympathetic and permissive in their dealings with abusive parents, and in their attempts to offer help. Conversely, in my experience in Cleveland, recognition that an offence had been committed led some police officers to take up an unyielding stance on prosecution. Neither response was particularly helpful to the abused or the abuser and both reinforced reluctance in medical and nursing professionals to take action. This situation improved over the years due to a gradual and tentative building of experience and trust between social workers, police, and health professionals, linked to multi-disciplinary opportunities for training and discussion. However, the fragile reality of

'working together' can be seen in moments of crisis
tion work, including Cleveland.

Working Together

Butler-Sloss (1988, P.13) describes the developing co-operation between
agencies who worked to increase awareness prior to the 1987 crisis. In cases
of physical abuse, records demonstrated 'effective operation of the child
abuse guidelines, good inter-agency and multi-disciplinary working and
sensitive social work practice'. A continuing programme of child abuse
training for all nurses had been extended and intensified. Much time was
given to talking to professional and lay people about parenting and its
associated problems and pressures, looking at situations common to most
families where children could be hurt. Most people with experience of
parenthood readily accept that occasionally even the most loving father or
mother under extremes of pressure could hit their child too hard, or strike
or throw a persistently crying baby. With knowledge and understanding
of the nature of abuse, and pre-disposing conditions, punitive attitudes can
soften to allow help to be offered without rejection of the abuser. This can
give both parent and professional confidence to seek help. As the climate
changed, slowly but very surely, there was a noticeable rise in identification
and referrals of injuries and neglect. Cases were referred at an earlier stage,
when bruising was of a less serious nature and could be seen as highlighting
a problem, examining background indicators and stressors, and finding
ways to enable the family to prevent further injury to the child. The shared
belief systems and frameworks for practice which were being established
were shaken to the foundations by the shock that sexual abuse could be anal
abuse of young children.

Searching for a Framework

A major event in the progress of child protection work in Cleveland was
a two day-symposium on child sexual abuse held at Teeside Polytechnic
in June 1984. This was a watershed for many professionals whose changed
understanding of child sexual abuse significantly influenced practice. All
professionals involved in child protection and workers from voluntary
agencies were represented. The effect was stunning. Most people would
rather avoid the subject as it is disturbing and distasteful, affecting us in

xpected ways. It may trigger off hidden memories of personal experiences which may be traumatic and distressing. It can 'knit' together strands of knowledge, suspicion and feeling, making us face up to things 'known' but not acknowledged. Those involved in counselling recalled clients describing incidents of sexual assault. These clients expressed feelings of shame, guilt, helplessness, inadequacy, poor self esteem and anger, tending to blame themselves. Some attempted suicide, mutilated themselves with knives or razor blades, or sought oblivion in drugs or alcohol. Yet somehow we couldn't make the quantum leap to believe that similar incidents of abuse could be happening in families with whom we were currently involved. It was acceptable to see bruises, and to assess growth and development when children might be neglected, but difficult to believe that known adults could or would sexually abuse their own or other people's children. As one community police sergeant remarked, ashen faced, 'My God! When I think of all the runaways I have rounded up and returned home without question . . . One could sense the shock waves as people absorbed the reality and considered the possibility of ongoing abuse in families they knew. '

The major criticism of all inquiry reports is of poor communication and coordination between agencies and professionals. Following publication of the Maria Colwell inquiry (1974), the DHSS recommended that Area Review Committees (ARCs) should be set up to oversee the management of all child abuse cases, to review the machinery for referrals and set up procedures to ensure that suspected cases of child abuse were correctly notified and dealt with. The Cleveland ARC was set up with a wide membership of senior representatives from all agencies involved in child care and protection. Each agency began the task of instituting procedures which were compiled into a booklet which was regularly reviewed and updated. To ensure improved communication, the DHSS also recommended that each discipline should appoint a 'designated officer', to whom all instances of suspected abuse should be referred. They would act as a link with other agencies and a source of specialist information, advice and support for fieldworkers dealing with traumatic and stressful situations. Cleveland initially gave this responsibility to district nursing officers. As the volume of referrals and subsequent case conferences increased, this was devolved to senior nursing officers. New posts were created in each health district. Other agencies also appointed designated officers. The police appointed a chief inspector in the community relations department to this post, but after two years this post was also devolved to district level. Social services, the education department, NSPCC and probation services also designated officers at area level. The designated officer group formed a second tier, which in contrast to the ARC comprised mostly people in day to day contact with abuse work. The ARC met twice a year, the designated officers more often to formulate progressive methods of working together, review documents and inquiry reports, and share new ideas and information in the field of child abuse. Good interdisciplinary working relationships were fostered by the process of working together at case conferences, liaising on suspected cases, and via joint training courses. Understanding and appreciation of each other's role, responsibilities, capabilities and agency function developed over time.

Seeds of Conflict

Growing awareness and increased identification of possible abuse cases led the ARC to agree a special category for sexual abuse on the register of children known to be at risk. A working party was set up to devise special procedures for dealing with sexual abuse for this purpose. Nursing designated officers attending case conferences throughout Cleveland had a unique overview of procedures, case conferences, case management and contact with a variety of professionals over a wide area. Since one concern was training, a working group was set up to assess levels of professional and community awareness, and to assess needs for information, training and support. Representatives were invited from all relevant groups. There was no response from child psychiatry, paediatrics, and little response from the education department, police and police surgeons. Social services and community nursing services appeared to be the only groups undertaking regular, ongoing training in sexual abuse. Social workers in education used the resources of the social service department but in neither sphere did fieldworkers have sufficient knowledge or information. School teachers were in industrial dispute and despite close daily contact with children had received no formal training in sexual abuse. Foster parent, child minders, playgroup leaders and nursery nurses all requested more information on the subject. Pressure of work made it difficult for hospital nursing staff on paediatric and gynaecological wards and accident and emergency units to attend lectures and talks. Consequently, they felt unprepared when sexually abused children were admitted to hospital. When approached, gynaecologists, general practitioners and some paediatricians admitted that they sometimes suspected abuse of children but did nothing. For example, some doctors were reluctant to see certain bruises as significant or to consider the proven link between physical and sexual abuse as a reason for looking at bottoms routinely as part of an overall examination. Without support from doctors, confidentiality of hospital records meant that some nurses felt unable to act on suspicions. A questionnaire circulated among groups of professional and voluntary workers showed that most felt the need for more basic information about abuse; how to recognise it, and what to do about suspicions. Some wanted help on how to listen and whom they should tell if a child tried to disclose abuse. At that time there was no provision for educating community groups and it was left to individual professionals and groups like Rape Crisis to talk to secondary school children and women in the community about sexual abuse and prevention. There was little enthusiasm at the designated officers group for setting up wider training, community education and prevention. It was feared that if the subject was aired too freely and publicly it could result in a rush of disclosures which would overwhelm existing resources. One rationale advanced was that we had barely reached stage five in Kempe's continuum of recognition of abuse and were not yet ready to take on prevention.

Developing Professional and Community Awareness

Those professionals at a more advanced stage of awareness were encouraged by the increased public interest shown by television programmes such as 'Childwatch' which in 1986 highlighted sexual abuse and resulted in the setting up of 'Childline', a telephone helpline for child victims. Intensive coverage at prime viewing time forced people to listen to children talking of their experiences. This could no longer be dismissed as lies, exaggeration, or fantasy. It led some adults to recall previously suppressed childhood incidents, and to re-experience the pain and trauma of the past. This resulted in an increasing rate of referral by teachers, school nurses, nursery teachers and nurses, mothers, and by the children themselves. In general there was a willingness to report suspicions in the knowledge that they would be investigated and dealt with as sensitively as possible. Young children's graphic accounts of abuse were believed. Medical examination was rarely carried out because of the type of abuse alleged, or the time that had elapsed since the incident. For example, a mother reported abuse of her daughter by her cohabitee. The police were satisfied after questioning the girl that she was telling the truth. She was allowed to go home overnight as the cohabitee had left, but he returned and by morning the girl and her mother retracted their statements. So strongly did the police believe the child's original story that despite lack of evidence or a medical diagnosis of abuse, an inspector went to the juvenile court to lay these concerns before the magistrates, who granted the local authority an order. A climate was being created in which children grew confident that adults would listen and believe what they had to say. Referrals increased at an alarming rate. The lack of therapeutic resources within Cleveland meant that children were taken when necessary to a child psychiatrist outside the area. Out of the three health districts, only one had a clinical child psychologist. One senior community medical officer who was able to offer therapeutic counselling to children was soon over-whelmed by numbers.

In 1986 Cleveland social services responded to the report of the Jasmine Beckford inquiry (1986) by appointing a child abuse consultant, Sue Richardson. She initiated a review of procedures and carried out an ongoing review of case conference recommendations and registrations. Figures for the last quarter of 1985 compared with the corresponding period in 1986 showed an increase in cases from 34 to 58 (sexual), 130 to 134 (physical), 26 to 46 (emotional and neglect) and 78 to 132 ('at risk' and multiple abuse). The large number of children registered as 'at risk' was partly due to an increasing number of convicted child abusers leaving prison and returning to live in families with children. Registration also included children considered to be at risk from relatives or unprotected because parents had denied the possibility of abuse. By the end of 1986, referrals, mainly of suspected sexual abuse, increased so much that it became difficult to arrange case conferences. It is worth noting that even under this pressure, multi-disciplinary case conferences were dealing with all categories of abuse without causing local disturbance or outrage. Where the child was believed by the parent there was no need to remove the child from home. It was practice in one district to hold a diagnostic conference asking for contributions from those with knowledge and information about the child and family, which would be gathered and assessed, and where decisions would be made as to the need for a full initial case conference. It was also practice to invite and involve parents wherever possible. Although this created stress for everyone concerned this continued in sexual abuse cases where it was felt appropriate. One of the main difficulties in confronting the problem of child sexual abuse was the different levels off acceptance of it among professionals and lay people as a serious problem for children which could be carried over into adulthood. However, those who were intimately involved with children's or adult(s) childhood experiences of abuse could not doubt the truth of what they heard. It was different for people at a senior level in agencies, who did not see sexual abuse as a problem and were not prepared to increase resources. In an attempt to increase awareness, seminars were held for health service managers, others involved in finance, psychiatrists, professions allied to medicine, members of the Community Health Council, and the editor of the local newspaper. By the end of 1986 all professions were struggling to cope with a significant increase in identification of sexual abuse, but management responded with disbelief. In January 1987, Dr Higgs joined the paediatric team at Middlesborough General hospital. Throughout the early months of 1987 the steady increase of referrals of sexual abuse continued.

The Developing Crisis

In response to the DHSS document 'Working Together' (DHSS, 1986) the new Joint Child Abuse Committee (JCAC) replaced ARC. It was to be accountable to existing Joint Consultative Committees (JCCs) between the health and local authorities. This was complicated in Cleveland because of the three separate health districts involved and their lack of agreement over issues. (Butler-Sloss, 1988, P.53). The JCAC had set up a new working party to review procedures for dealing with child protection. When draft procedures were circulated, wide variations in practice between professionals again became apparent where belief systems were at different stages. for example, the reason given for few referrals of sexual abuse in one district was that it was a close-knit community where a great deal of preventative work was done. (Butler-Sloss, 1988, P. 111). Here, the paediatrician did not regard themselves as having special expertise and were not prepared to be named as the best person to examine a child suspected of having been abused. Few cases were referred to them and children were seen by police surgeons. Police arguments about who was best equipped to examine children, where this examination should take place, and whether social workers could jointly investigate suspected cases remained unresolved. The police representative was withdrawn from the last meeting of the working party and in his absence the group agreed new procedures, giving paediatrician a major role. (Butler-Sloss, 1988, P. 95-96). This was criticised in the inquiry report and with hindsight, it was a measure of people's frustration that the procedures were agreed this way. By this time, there had been a confrontation between police surgeon and paediatrician which resulted in the issuing of a police internal memorandum calling into question the medical findings of Dr Higgs in respect of child sexual abuse and requesting caution in proceeding without corroborating evidence (Butler-Sloss, 1988. pp 51 and 95). This was not communicated to the social services department directly, neither did social services tell the police that they would in future refuse access to the police surgeon. (Butler-Sloss, 1988, P. 95). At a local level this affected relationships within case conferences – police would not accept any diagnosis made by Dr Higgs without corroborative evidence and therefore few investigations were pursued. Parents were told to ignore diagnoses by Dr Higgs. Failure to carry out investigations further fragmented relationships between social workers and police.

All activity was centred on Middlesborough General Hospital. Because of the sheer numbers of children being examined and admitted to the paediatric wards, communication systems broke down. Designated officers were no longer informed of suspicions about children in their areas (Butler-Sloss, 1988, P.127). Without the possibility of immediate liaison between designated officers, case conferences were delayed as it took longer to investigate and gather information. Health visitors, general practitioners and school nurses were approached by frantic parents asking for explanations and help. Nursing staff who coped magnificently with epidemics of illness found themselves struggling with belief as numbers of children soared. (Butler-Sloss, 1988, P.127). They were under extreme pressure from distressed, angry and sad parents, apparently abandoned by social workers who were themselves stretched to breaking point, and from children they saw as well and disruptive in a ward of sick children. (Butler-Sloss, 1988, P.127).

The greatest challenge for us all as the crisis progressed was to resist denial. Many times we had to reflect and remind ourselves of what we knew from experience, but even this knowledge became harder to handle as the numbers of children diagnosed grew. We know with hindsight that the same rate of reporting was occurring elsewhere e.g. Leeds and Lancashire, but at the same time connections were not being made between one area and another. There were feelings of helplessness, anger and frustration, mirroring those of children and parents. We feared that the progress made in child protection over six years in Cleveland had gone without trace and that the great danger for children was that people would no longer believe them or in the reality of sexual abuse. We feared that victims and families would no longer trust social workers to respond appropriately. We were concerned that child psychiatry could not give support to professional staff, take a role in diagnosis or agree on the best treatment of child victims. (Butler-Sloss, 1988, pp 153-154). In an after dinner speech Butler-Sloss, (1989) spoke of the Cleveland inquiry and commented on the fact that so few children told a story prior to being medically examined. One who did, over a two year period, tell the child psychiatrist, was disbelieved about the serious abuse being inflicted on him by his father. This eleven year old had a degree of mental handicap and was thought to be fantasising. The public judgement given later by Justice Sheldon was that both the boy and his young sister had been sexually abused for a number of years and praised Dr Wyatt for bringing the case to attention. Child psychiatrists have subsequently been involved on the JCAC and in child abuse work.

General practitioners rarely attend case conferences. Those who did attend could be inhibited by the presence of parents who were also their responsibility as patients. This meant that much important medical information was unavailable to case conferences except through the health visitor. (Butler-Sloss, 1988, P.157). Health visitors too were faced with distraught parents to whom they had no information to give.

The JCAC was still struggling to agree a constitution and membership in the early months of 1987 and was in no position to give help as the first disagreements between police and doctors developed. The old ARC had expired from natural causes just at the time that the 'Working Together' document was published, giving an opportunity to start afresh rather than attempt to resuscitate the ARC. An enthusiastic core group tried to move forward but as more and more procedural disagreements arose, there was insufficient executive power to achieve progress. (Butler-Sloss, 1988, pp 53–54). Both the ARC and the JCAC were looked at with jaundiced eyes by social services managers who had to carry out procedures and the new committee was swiftly and significantly christened 'The Jackass'.

The effect of the crisis on agencies followed the pattern of previous inquiry situations. Even before the official announcement on 9th June 1987, senior managers had taken over and from that time excluded designated officers from planning and decision making. Individual agencies closed ranks for protection. Documents and records were called in for the inquiry and statements had to be prepared.

Following the events of early 1987 and disagreement between paediatrician and police surgeon, the police had set up a special unit to deal with suspected sexual abuse. Instead of each individual district carrying out its own investigation, all referrals were passed to this unit. This was helpful in that it ensured a common policy throughout Cleveland but it also helped to concentrate the power of the police to deal with situations unilaterally. (Butler-Sloss, 1988, p.81) describes how Cleveland Constabulary were 'slow to respond' to the need for 'more complex and sensitive type of interagency intervention'. They were reluctant to alter existing arrangements and 'saw themselves as the sole agency charged with the investigation of sexual offences against children'. It also meant that the emphasis was on hard evidence rather than using the wider balance of probability which had previously been so helpful to the abused child.

The media took a very partisan stance, allying themselves to parents, police and MP. Biased television programmes which were shown as 'factual' gave parent's stories with no recourse for professionals to counter inaccuracies. The media were used extensively by Stuart Bell MP in his campaign to support parents. He brought the crisis situation to the attention of the media and parliament. He made 'intemperate and inflammatory remarks' and several serious allegations and criticisms which the inquiry examined and rejected. (Butler-Sloss, 1988, pp163,and 166–8).

What must have been particularly difficult for the key figures in the crisis to bear was avoidance by some colleagues who distanced themselves for fear that they would be 'contaminated' and their work discredited if they offered support. Some professionals suggested that their own systems could have handled things different and better. Others working with child sexual abuse tended to keep their heads down and dissociate themselves. Managers were not always supportive. They did not appreciate the realities of the problems or perhaps doubted the information they were given. Also they had their own problems!

As a result of differences of opinion and belief about the existence, incidence and long term effects of sexual abuse, people tended to take up polarised positions. This is illustrated by Hawkins and Shohet (1989, pp129–30). In their triangular model of 'persecutor', 'victim' and 'rescuer', initially the parents were seen as 'persecutors', children as 'victims' and doctors and social services as 'rescuers'. Following the massive outcry from parents, the local MP and the media, positions on the triangle shifted to doctors being persecutors of families as victims, with the media and the local MP as rescuers. The rescuers then turned on the persecutors, calling for their dismissal and painting them as evil, rather than dedicated professionals trying to do their jobs. The triangle then became persecutor (media and local MP), victim (doctors and social services), and the new rescuer (the inquiry report). However it seems that the Butler-Sloss report did not resolve these problems which still prevent society accepting and dealing with child sexual abuse.

Conclusion

The Inquiry Report was welcomed by the majority of people because it acknowledged the problem of child sexual abuse, saw the need to recognise and describe the extent of it and to establish more accurate data. It pointed out that children should not be seen merely as objects of adult concern but as individuals. The report stressed the importance of interagency agreement in the common aim of identifying and helping abused children, and endorsed the part played by particular professionals, such as doctors, in initiating concern on behalf of the child. It also raised many dilemmas for case management,

In the post-Cleveland years, we have learned of rituals involving the sexual and emotional abuse of children. Child molesters have been reported visiting homes, posing as social workers or health visitors and trying to examine children. NSPCC figures (1990) show a thirty-five percent increase in children on 'at risk' registers with one hundred percent increase in emotional abuse, sixty-two percent increase in neglect, sixty-six percent in 'grave concern', fifteen percent in physical abuse, and a four percent increase in sexual abuse. Senior police officers were told at their annual conference in 1990 that something must be done about paedophiles who could admit to molesting in excess of two hundred children when caught. Cleveland Child Protection Committee was reported (Evening Gazette May 10th 1990) to state that sexual abuse referrals were at roughly

the same level as before the crisis. The public were *r*
abuse was being handled well since no cases had *b*
special panel) because of professional disagreemen*
statement in the same news item is that the experts had stᴉᴉᴉ ..
the best way to provide facilities for examining and interviewing cᴉᴉᴉ..
and families in Cleveland.

Fairly uniform national procedures for co-operative action have been
developed to protect children within the statutory legal framework.
However, considerable differences of approach remain from one area to
another. Doctors may still be reluctant to report over chastisement or other
abuse of children for fear of unleashing a juggernaut which could run out
of control. One could speculate that they and other groups of workers
involved with children and families would be even more reluctant to pass
on concerns or suspicions of sexual abuse, especially after the media
reporting of events in Cleveland. Clouds of misinformation still blur the
important issues for professionals and allow the public to dismiss the
problem as having been grossly inflated. It is extremely difficult to show
the true incidence of the sexual abuse of children, which is wrapped in
secrecy. Summit (1988, p.41) points out that 'it is all of society, not just the
immediately affected, that protects the secret of child sexual abuse'. The
Pigot report (1989) notes a large national increase of children on child
protection registers but relatively small numbers of attempted prosecutions
and even smaller numbers of successful ones. Cleveland has been isolated,
frozen in time, its lessons contained and curtailed, a message to others not
to lift the stone.

2 A Framework of Belief

Sue Richardson and Heather Bacon

If we are to retain our belief in a child -centred approach, then we cannot totally protect the adult's rights of justice at the same time. A compromise must be decided upon and adhered to when pressures mount to shift the balance away from the child towards the adult.
(J. Sloan and J. Murdoch, 1990)

Introduction

We have learned from our experience in Cleveland that effective work in child protection needs to be grounded in a clear, explicit and shared belief system which can form the foundation for inter-agency agreement and cooperation. Whilst recognizing that child sexual abuse is a complex problem, requiring a sophisticated and sensitive model for intervention, we wish to emphasize those aspects which centrally concern the child's state, the child's response to intervention and the obligations we have as adults towards the child. At the same time, we accept the view of the Cleveland inquiry that 'a child's needs and best interests cannot be fully considered in isolation from knowledge about, and full understanding of, all the circumstances relating to its parents' (Butler-Sloss,1988 p.75). An assumption has emerged from Cleveland that 'patterns of professional practice which alienate parents and isolate children at the centre of conflict' (Butler-Sloss, 1988 p.75) can eventually be superseded by an approach which, while being child-centred, recognizes that parents and children have equal rights. In striving for this goal, we recognize that at present children's rights are not given equal weight, particularly within the legal system. For this reason, we believe that a healthy balance between

17

children's and adults' rights can be achieved only by placing more weight on the side of the child until the present imbalance is redressed. In this book we address ways in which all adults, not only those involved in child protection work, can help to shift this balance through a process of child advocacy.

Several writers (e.g.Finkelhor, 1986, Tiernay and Corwin, 1983, Glaser and Frosch, 1988, La Fontaine, 1990) have expressed concern about the absence of a uniformly accepted operational definition of child sexual abuse. A consensus will not be achieved until an adequate working knowledge base is available. As practitioners, we feel it is essential to broaden the concept of abuse beyond the strictly forensic approach adopted for legal and research purposes. Our argument is based on the assumption that any interaction which distorts and disrupts the child's development will always be harmful (Finkelhor, 1986, Wyatt and Powell, 1988). Such behaviours are not adequately described by medical or overt behavioral indicators. As Bolton et. al. (1989) emphasize in their framework of 'abuse of sexuality', an abusive experience is part of an interaction with an adult and the child's stage of development must be taken into account in assessing the effect the abuse will have. We find this approach more useful in determining protective and therapeutic responses than efforts to establish the form or degree of severity of any abusive acts. An underlying belief is that child sexual abuse is basically an abuse of adult power over children, primarily male power, although this does not preclude abuse by women. Because of children's powerlessness and dependence on adults, most abuse goes undetected for long periods with devastating long-term emotional and psychological consequences. Although some victims may be driven to perpetrate abuse on others, we know that this outcome is not inevitable, especially where help and protection are provided. We believe in the power of healing after even the most severe abuse. However, healing cannot begin until the reality of the abuse is openly acknowledged and victims are provided with an advocate who will believe them, be willing to hear their pain and take action to stop the abuse. Disclosure is therefore regarded as the first step in the healing process, despite the crisis it involves for the child, the family and helpers.

By 'disclosure' we mean 'the process whereby the abuse is brought to the attention of someone else besides the child and his or her abuser' (Jones and McQuiston 1988 p.2). This can be via an indirect 'open warning' (Ounsted and Lynch, 1976), by direct statements from the child or allegations by an adult, by physical signs, symptoms and illness or through behavioral indicators such as the child acting as a perpetrator towards others. The disclosure, which may not coincide with the abuse, can be made at any stage in childhood or delayed until adulthood. In acting as an advocate for the child, we believe adults should seek to take the responsibility for disclosure. To intervene effectively, the advocate needs an authoritative mandate which is supported and understood by the community. Child advocacy involves a willingness to engage in creative conflict with adult interests because the rights of the child are unequally represented in our society.

The Advocate's Role

In a laudable attempt to redress the balance in favour of children's rights, organizations such as Childline and the Samaritans base their work on the belief, endorsed in the Cleveland report, that when 'an abused child does not choose to tell . . . the adults should respect that view' (Butler-Sloss, 1988 p.207). However, although the disclosure process may be hazardous for the child, we feel that adults should act in the child's long term interests where necessary. Children can only make judgements based on their developmental stage and readiness for adult intervention. Whilst we understand the fear of discounting the child's rights, we believe that the child should not carry the responsibility of deciding what should happen.

Society recognizes a wide range of situations in which children are unable to give informed consent. Children are unable to appreciate the potentially damaging consequences for their adult mental health if the abuse remains undisclosed. We subscribe to Miller's view (1985 p.184) that 'An unacknowledged trauma is like a wound that never heals over and can start to bleed again at any time. In a supportive environment the wound can become visible and finally heal completely'. Miller's work argues convincingly that 'Not being able to talk about or even *know* about these wounds is what later leads to pathological developments'(Miller, 1985, p.126; author's italics). Her work shows that the silenced, suffering child cannot speak out and requires an advocate who may have to reject prevailing adult values, identify completely with the child and provide the necessary healing and supportive environment.

Miller's writings are not designed to address the practice implications for work with abused children. In our application of the principles which

19

she sets out, the implication is that adults should take responsibility for the child who should not be left to make his or her own way up the continuum described in Chapter 5. This task is impossible for many children, as the testimony of adult survivors shows. We are committed to developing forms of intervention which do not necessarily depend on the child's testimony. Restricting ourselves to reactive practice leaves an inappropriate degree of responsibility with children. Increased awareness of alerting signs and symptoms, together with developments in medical diagnosis, can provide a wider range of options to initiate action on their behalf. An integral part of the intervention should be to provide protection from the adverse consequences of disclosure, such the crisis for the family and pressure to retract. We agree with Harrop (1990) that intervention means 'correctly identifying abusive situations, and limiting interventions to the least needed to stop the abuse whilst seeking to restore the child's selfworth'. Successful intervention from the child's point of view will almost always involve offering therapy to the child and/or support for the child's carer in dealing with the effects of the abuse. Rather than avoiding the crisis and dilemmas of intervention altogether, a child–centred approach would minimize sources of secondary victimization of the child which could result from the disclosure process. In an ideal world, it would not be so hard to achieve what children often want : to retain the 'good' parts of the relationship with the abuser while preventing further abuse. As it is, the over-riding concern must be to stop the abuse. We acknowledge that this may be at a cost to the child. The view (Butler-Sloss, 1988, p.7) that the abuser rather than the child should be removed would go some way towards lessening the trauma for some children. However, this strategy does not apply to all groups of children, particularly not to those described as group B in Chapter 3, where the doctor may be the first to raise the concern and the abuser is unknown. Rather than seek stratagems which will inevitably break down in individual cases, we suggest that the principles of child advocacy which we have outlined provide a guiding philosophy from which to devise intervention tailored to the individual child.

The United Nations Convention on the Rights of the Child (1989) accepts the child's right to be protected from exploitation and abuse. The Convention is based on the principle 'That children need special safeguards beyond those provided to adults' (Unicef, 1988). Advocacy for the child can provide a crucial safeguard to ensure that the dilemmas of intervention are resolved in favour of the child. In relation to the inner and outer reality of the abused child, the advocate's role is described by Southgate (1989) as that of nurturer, witness, protester, translator and supporter of the victim's inner strength and creativity. This vision is based primarily on the work of Alice Miller (1983, 1985 and 1987), whose writings expose the reality of child abuse, its historical denial or concealment by adults and its far reaching implications in the context of social attitudes to child rearing. The advocate has almost identical tasks, whether working with the wounded inner child within an adult or with an actual child. In the latter case, the advocate bears a different degree of responsibility to intervene and stop the abuse, which by definition children are too powerless to do for themselves.

Wells (1990, p.58) says that the task of the practitioner in a child- centred model is to say five things to the child: I believe you; I am glad you came to me; I am sorry this has happened; it is not your fault; together we are going to do something to get some help. There are then five things to do: listen; believe and let the child know this; affirm whatever feelings the child has; refer to and follow procedures; follow up and support the child. The therapist is instructed to switch off adult agendas and enter the child's world. This is an active model in which the adult must strive to find a way to bridge the gap between the child's inner world and the adult world where the child's needs for protection must be addressed.

There are frequent conflicts within and between professional networks, for example paediatricians/police surgeons, social workers/legal advisors, child psychiatrists/judges, which can distract from the child centred approach to investigation capable of ensuring that advocacy is provided for the child. In many instances disclosure may be most likely to take place during investigation if the child and protective members of the family can be supported. For those children who are unable to disclose spontaneously, especially very young children, medical or other windows into the child's predicament should be utilized. The concept of the medical window, where the doctor may be the only person able to act as the child's advocate, has been largely misunderstood by commentators on the Cleveland crisis. For example, Wattam (1989) comments that the definition of child sexual abuse in Cleveland i.e .a medical one, is far too narrow, centring largely on incest and anal abuse and putatively medical symptoms. The role of the paediatrician as the child's advocate is argued in Chapter 3.

We recognize a dilemma in that some children can only be unlocked

21

from the abuse if the helper can enter their inner world at a pace the child can manage, without using powerful interventions, which it can be argued, mirror the abuse. The purpose of authoritative intervention is to create the psychological and emotional space the child needs to work through the disclosure process. By authoritative intervention, we mean the use of a mandate, derived from child protection legislation, or given by a non-abusing parent, or a combination of the two. The purpose is to structure and control the process of investigation and protection in favour of the child. It must be allied with the presence of an advocate who can focus on the child's needs and is perceived as doing so by the child. When this can be provided, we reject the view, arising from popular myths about Cleveland, that children need 'protection from protection'(HMSO 1990, 1.33) or that authoritative intervention is bound to mirror the dynamics of abuse. We agree with Sgroi (1984, pp.82-83) that 'effective intervention into a disordered power system can only be accomplished in an authoritative fashion and from a position of power; other intervention methodologies invite the offender to misuse power further to suppress the allegation, to undermine the child's credibility and to ward off interference'.

Authoritative intervention remains humane where it is based on an alliance with the child and protective members of the child's family. Non-abusing family members, particularly mothers, are potentially the most important advocates for the child, especially if it is recognized that they too may need an advocate of their own. During the Cleveland crisis, polarization between professionals and parents resulted when over-stretched resources meant that insufficient help and support was available. This problem was eased by the opening of a Child Resource Centre where mothers could be supported (Richardson, 1989). Some women were able to protect their children, sometimes in defiance of court decisions. Our concern about the influence of the prevailing social context for judicial decision-making means that we must ensure that the authority invested in protective family members is equally powerful. We therefore see an alliance of advocates as the best means of protecting the child. We would like to see the Cleveland inquiry's concept of authority expanded from the view that 'Ultimately children can only be protected on the basis of evidence which can be tested in Court' (Butler-Sloss, 1988 p.73). The problem of relying on the adversarial legal situation to shape intervention on behalf of the child is discussed by Pigot (1989). Despite moves towards reform, we

22

see the legal forum as inevitably operating to adult agendas in which the definition of child abuse and decisions on protection are influenced by the prevailing political and social climate. The lack of consensus between professionals and the courts is illustrated by a decision in the Court of Appeal (Re P (minors)), Lords Justice Nourse and Russell and Sir Roualeyn Cumming Bruce, 25th October 1990). In this case, the court turned down the local authority's appeal against an order providing for a stepfather's return to the home after having been held to have sexually abused his nine year old stepdaughter. The solicitor for the local authority was held to have been in serious contempt of court for instructing a social worker to persuade the stepfather not to avail himself of his right of staying access pending the appeal hearing. Difficult dilemmas arise when the requirements of the courts and what is considered to be good child care practice do not correspond. Some of the implications are explored in Chapters 6 and 8.

Children's Rights

Children's rights are unequally represented in our society. This is reflected in the legal system, in which Pigot (1989, pp.66–67) suggests that a 'fundamental change of attitude towards children in the legal context is required' to address the problem of children's evidence and reduce 'the near certainty of immunity from prosecution for those who abuse small children in private'. Because power is an inherent issue, a legal framework is often an important basis of advocacy for the child but should be founded on believing the child, a realistic appraisal of perpetrator behaviour and knowledge of how children are forced to accommodate to abuse. Following events in Cleveland, there has been much concern that legal justification for intervention can be misplaced. Some reassurance can be gained from the Official Solicitor (Levy, 1989 p.89), who concludes from the interviews his officers conducted with the children that 'One of my lasting impressions of Cleveland will be the many accounts, often extremely harrowing, of sexual abuse at the hands of often trusted adults and the frequently expressed gratitude and relief at the intervention of the medical experts and social services in Cleveland'. In the U.K., legal changes have ensued which are designed to reduce the scope for such intervention and attempt to reconcile opposing interests and philosophies. In commenting on the 1989 Children Act, Bainham (1990) points out that there is a fundamental conflict between a commitment to the welfare principle in respect of children and holding a policy of non-intervention by the state in family life. He suggests that these two basically incongruous principles can only be reconciled where parents accept their responsibilities as well as their rights. When this breaks down, 'The danger of having an over-arching principle or philosophy of non – intervention is that children's interests will become too closely identified with those of their parents and that the role of the state, in protecting the individual interests of children, will be undermined' (Bainham, 1990 p 145).

A child centred approach means making a space in which children are listened to and believed and their interests protected in a way which allows them to feel safe and trusting enough to unburden. Butler-Sloss (1988,p 204) cites the view of the Royal College of Psychiatrists, who 'felt that a statement by the child that sexual abuse has occurred should be taken seriously, but you are pre-judging the issue if you say you believe it –.' On the other hand, the report also quotes DHSS guidelines (1986) that 'A child's statement that he or she is being abused should be taken as true until proved otherwise' (Butler-Sloss, 1988 p 204). The inquiry was reminded by Bentovim that 'The child is entitled to belief' (Butler-Sloss, 1988 p 204). The stance adopted by many courts and practitioners since the publication of the Cleveland report is that 'What any child says must be listened to and taken seriously, but the professionals must be very careful not to prejudge the issue' (Re E Minor, Family Division, Mr Justice Scott Baker, The Independent, 27th March 1990). We do not feel that these differences of opinion have yet been reconciled and are concerned about their impact on the child's absolute right to be protected from abuse.

In this context of conflicting beliefs, children's statements are often disregarded in favour of the perpetrator's denial. The grounds given are often that there is insufficient evidence from the child itself or no corroboration. A series of authoritative sources including, for example, the Pigot Committee (1989), have expressed concern that the English criminal justice system is often weighted against the child and open to exploitation by abusers. This committee recommended fundamental changes in the rules for children's evidence, such as abolishing the rule that children could not be regarded as competent witnesses, which had been an obstacle for children everywhere, including Cleveland. Ewbank re G Minors (Ewbank, 1988) illustrates the difficulties which can otherwise arise. A little girl of five years had alerted her mother by a comment. The mother was seen as unreliable because she was suing for divorce. An older brother had disclosed repeated sodomy by his father, with medical findings which the police surgeon stated could be consistent with this. The judge said that there was no corroboration of any weight of the mother's story. The boy was disbelieved, the judge concluding that 'the child's remarks were brought on by a competitive urge' to be better than his sister. He summed up: 'The mother – – – is likely to go on believing that sexual abuse has taken place whatever decision the court makes – – – I have come to the conclusion that there are no grounds for denying access to the father – – – it will have to be supervised, firstly to safeguard the father from further allegations of sexual abuse and secondly to give some reassurance to the mother' (Ewbank, 1987 p.320). Whatever the truth of the matter, the children's needs seem to have been overlooked and the children, with their mother, discredited. Mothers who believe and report what their children say can thus often be placed in 'double jeopardy' (MacFarlane, 1986 p 149) in relation to future custody of their children. They may be automatically regarded as 'paranoid, hysterical or perverted' for suspecting abuse, in contrast to the 'seemingly rational and caring father' seen as incapable of the behaviours described.

There are many factors which militate against children in courts, some of which have been addressed by Pigot:

> 'in other parts of the world, where the quality of justice is not inferior to our own, listening to what very small children have to say and providing suitable means for children to describe their experiences – – – is not regarded as unusual, unreasonable, or a threat to the principle that the prosecution must discharge the burden of proof.' (Pigot, 1989 p 6)

Every legal and procedural improvement appears beset by difficulties and contradictions. For example, the use of certain camera techniques in videotaping the evidence of child victims has been shown in a psychologists' study to distort adult perceptions of what the children say (Westcott et al, 1990). One American state, in an effort to eliminate adult bias, has introduced robots to interview children. We do not believe that there can be any mechanistic alternative to the presence and commitment of a child-centred advocate who can ensure that the child's voice is heard. In a context where so many factors prevent the child being listened to, the advocate's role cannot be neutral. However, this stance has the effect of raising conflict within a system biased towards adults. La Fontaine (1990 p 232) reminds us that: 'Until we all abandon the dogma of parents' natural infallibility, children will continue to be sexually abused and to despair of getting help'.

Much concern was generated in Cleveland about parent's rights. There seemed to be a dichotomy which meant that somebody had to be wrong, or lying, and that this person should forfeit his or her rights once this became clear. Thus, faced with a child who alleged abuse by the father and a father who strenuously denied this, most onlookers and participants naturally tended to assume that someone was lying. In the controversy, adult's voices were louder than children's. Further confusion arose when children were unable to say whether or not they were being abused, or when they denied the abuse in the presence of evidence to the contrary. Inevitably, this produced polarization of the argument, at the expense of both the child and the alleged or unknown perpetrator, and powerful pressures were then generated to find an alternative explanation. If the medical evidence could be discredited or ignored, the choice about what to believe could be avoided. Simple common sense hardly ever found a voice. Had the crime of attempted murder been at issue, the accused would be understood as more likely to deny the crime than the victim to make up the allegation or the investigator's judgement to be at fault, particularly if there were medical evidence of assault. Yet the alleged perpetrators were rarely accused of lying, in contrast to the children and their professional advocates who were portrayed as making it up. An equivalent process in the legal system meant that, in the name of human rights, the child – orientated 'balance of probabilities' test used in civil law was superseded by the application of the tenet of criminal law 'beyond all reasonable doubt'. The rationale for this has been explicitly stated by Judge Sheldon who ruled that:

> 'a higher degree of probability is required to satisfy the court that the father has been guilty of some sexual misconduct with his daughter than would be needed to justify the conclusion that the child has been the victim of some such behaviour of whatever nature and whoever may have been its perpetrator.' (Butler-Sloss, 1988 p.232)

It is hard to understand legal rulings such as these without the explanation that they are fuelled by a denial process.

Dealing with Denial

Butler-Sloss (1988 p.82) comments that efforts in Cleveland to address the

26

issue of denial had 'the opposite effect'. That societal denial is a reality is detailed in a range of sources such as Rush (1980), Miller (1985) and Summit (1988). Developing awareness of the dimensions of abuse, including highly organized child sex rings and ritualistic practices, require a model for understanding. We suggest there are different levels of denial to be addressed: benign, transformed and malign. These can be taken to exist at both societal and individual level, at which different forms of intervention are indicated. Benign denial stems from both a lack of basic information and the initial stages of shock and disbelief which accompany a dawning understanding. To overcome it, the provision of information in a climate of open debate is helpful. At this level, community initiatives have an important role. Transformed denial is more complex, since it arises from a distorted form of knowledge. It can result from individuals themselves having suffered abuse, the pain of which remains hidden from their consciousness or is too difficult to acknowledge directly. It can also result from or be conflated by misinformation, like that put out during the hostile media campaigns about events in Cleveland (Illesley, 1990), parts of Europe (Jonka, 1989) and America (Summit, 1989). Menzie (1960) found in her research into nursing services in a general hospital that social defence systems were created as a defence against anxiety. These systems involved a range of responses and procedures within the individual and the institution. Their characteristic purpose was to avoid the experience of anxiety ,guilt, doubt and uncertainty' which was inevitably engendered by the task but was felt to be 'too deep and dangerous for full confrontation'. The problem of child sexual abuse by its nature evokes deep anxieties which can be too overwhelming to contemplate. Transformed denial is a more complex problem to address and involves an alliance with en-lightened sections of the community who can encourage public disclosure and honest debate.

Malign denial is more accurately a form of concealment, related to having a vested interest of some kind in promoting continued denial of the facts. This can take place at an individual level, typically the denial of a perpetrator facing society's retribution, or the denial resulting from the unresolved anguish of a non-abusing parent who would otherwise have to choose between their child and their partner. On a broader level, it can range from a District Health Authority's denial that events in Cleveland had caused a dramatic drop in referrals from doctors in the face of figures to the contrary (Evening Gazette, 12.4.90), to the destructive vested interests which profit from child sex rings and child pornography. At this societal level, a political response is needed, the nature of which will be influenced by the level of empowerment of the community.

The role of survivors in changing the dynamic deserves special consideration. Summit (1988, p.58) calls for 'a survivors revolt that will finally open our ears to children and open our eyes to the societal flaws which we have chosen to overlook'. His dreams of a coalition of protective forces throughout the whole community – investigative and treatment agencies, the justice system, families, self-help and survivor groups – require a new model of shared activity and practice which goes beyond procedural issues and crosses all boundaries. Only when a tri-partite alliance is formed between professionals, survivors and 'lay' members of the community can there be a mandate to intervene.

This alliance harnesses the energy inherent in the anger and pain of abuse. In Chapter 7 we examine how a community's informed support might be mobilized to avoid the sort of paralysis and hurt which characterized responses in Cleveland.

The Value of Conflict

Conflict is inherent both in the complex multi-disciplinary system and in the problem itself, which defies simple solutions. In our view, conflict can be useful and creative. The challenge it poses for the organization is examined in more detail by Richardson (1989, p.123) who also points out that there is bound to be 'a tension between the organization's need for control and the conditions in which professionals can survive and work creatively'. This lies in the nature of the problem and its unique ability to create dissension in communities, as outlined by Finkelhor et al (1984).

Conflict can be seen as part of a normal developmental process, which enables a genuine rather than a forced consensus to be forged. Anything other than this will tend to be fragile and break down when the system is placed under stress. Conflict makes implicit beliefs explicit and it may not be possible to assess the health of the system until this happens. At this stage, it can be expedient to retreat behind agency boundaries rather than be left with ownership of a problem which cannot be solved and which threatens existing social and professional hierarchies. There are strong pressures for consensus in every system and the scapegoating of individuals may be a preferred means of maintaining the status quo. Richardson and Bacon

(1988) have put forward an hypothesis suggesting the apparent advantages of conflict-avoidance by professionals outside Cleveland during the crisis: the NIOBY (not in our backyard) syndrome, which allowed conflicts to be redirected elsewhere. Butler-Sloss (1989, p.156) has commented that she 'did have the impression that Cleveland happened to be the battlefield of a wider war that was being fought round the country' and that 'It is sad that it took a situation in the North-East to shake people into the necessary degree of self-analysis and self-criticism. It is much easier to blame one's neighbour (1990,p.6)'.

Healthy conflict resolution is also inhibited by taboos, by the view that conflict itself is unprofessional and by the lack of both arbitration and truly neutral arbitrators. De Bono (1985) states that our very thinking about conflict is restricted by a lack of creative concepts or even a language in which conflict can be addressed. We suggest that the Cleveland inquiry acted as a conflict regulator at the expense of the creativity and child-centred risk taking which we see as the only way to tackle practice dilemmas.

Hill (1990) describes inquiries as having both manifest and latent purposes . Manifest lessons consist of direct findings and recommendations while latent functions are 'to appease public disquiet – – – and– – – define the nature and causation of child abuse in ways which detach it from wider social processes and responsibilities'. Inquiries can be based on either adversarial or inquisitorial methods in their task of establishing the 'truth'. The adversarial approach is characterized by legal methods of examination and cross- examination where parties called to give evidence are legally represented (as in Cleveland). The disadvantage is that the impact of a court-like atmosphere makes workers feel they are on trial (Hallet 1989). The Tyra Henry inquiry (1987) drew attention to the conflicting duties of legal representatives in assisting the inquiry and in protecting their clients' interests. Their report suggests that an inquisitorial approach helps witnesses to be more open in telling the panel things it needs to know, results in less stress and 'a lifting of the shadow that the inquiry casts over the lives of those centrally involved' (Henry, 1987, p.162)

Hallett (1990, p.134) points out that ' An interesting facet of the inquiries to date, including Cleveland, is that while many professions have been criticized, the activities of the legal profession and the working of the courts have generally gone unremarked'. Other professionals, particularly social workers, have been profoundly affected by inquiry findings which can be almost inseparable from disciplinary judgements. Butler-Sloss (1988

29

p.245) addressed this difficulty in expressing both the hope that 'the troubles of 1987 will recede for those concerned with the protection of children in Cleveland' and the view that 'criticisms of individuals should not be allowed to obscure the wider failings of agencies'. However, there are often no clear bench marks for practice and the media and the inquiry itself are likely to focus attention on frontline workers and avoid scrutinizing the underlying structure.

It is often public pressure that determines whether or not an inquiry is held but due to the problems outlined above, it may not provide a real basis for restoring public confidence. Professor Olive Stephenson (1988) is of the opinion that the role of any inquiry in educating the public is like 'educating them about the health service by a visit to the mortuary'. For these reasons, the process of any public inquiry is likely to stifle expression of the real conflicts which underlay the events. It cannot therefore be a vehicle for resolving them. Individuals and agencies are likely to be scapegoated and retreat to safe ground rather than insist that the real issues be kept open for debate. Few issues could be more dangerous to control in this way than child sexual abuse. The final report of the Social Services Inspectorate (1990) into the post-inquiry collaborative working arrangements between agencies in Cleveland enabled politicians and the media to endorse their view that 'Its now time to put the past behind us' (Virginia Bottomley, The Guardian, 8th June 1990). At the same time, the report confirms that there were 'indications – – – of a tendency to err in the favour of caution in referring to other agencies in some cases, perhaps related to the events leading up to the Butler-Sloss inquiry and previous SSI inspections'. This was accompanied by the release of figures by the Child Protection Committee confirming that there had been a radical drop since the crisis from 12% to 2% of total referrals in cases referred by hospitals (Evening Gazette 8th June 1990). One politician welcomed this trend as 'back to something like a normal level for sexual abuse' (Tim Devlin, Evening Gazette, 8th June 1990). This comment is indicative of an underlying political agenda of containment to match reduced resources in the public sector. Since even the most conservative estimates of prevalence indicate that the numbers of identified cases of sexual abuse are likely to be a gross underestimate, there are inevitably conflicting agendas. The President of the Association of Directors of Social Services, in his evidence to the Cleveland inquiry, said that 'The Cleveland case, of course, begs the question of how any Department

30

would cope logistically under a high bombardment rate' (Butler-Sloss, 1988 p.85). One year later, a Mori poll of all directors of social services (Community Care 1st June 1989) found that over three quarters of departments which responded said their resources were inadequate to cope with what was seen as the tip of the iceberg of child sexual abuse. The Cleveland experience illustrates many of the defence mechanisms which can ensue, including scapegoating and isolating the messengers, silencing the debate and relying on procedural systems designed to contain the problem within manageable proportions. The impetus is to 'draw a veil over the past' (Stuart Bell, Evening Gazette, 8th June 1990) and secure agreements which can trust the matter be 'buried in the mists of history' (Lord Donaldson, The Independent 25th April 1990). Discussion is seen as dangerous and any group attempting to continue the debate is likely to be labelled as destructive of calm and consensus. In our opinion, there are risks to children from a consensus amongst adults which may serve to mask the reality of abuse. La Fontaine (1990 p.220) reminds us that 'all too often the co-operation can become an end in itself and the question of how this can benefit the victim is forgotten'. Some conflicts cannot possibly be easily reconciled and premature attempts may be imposed at the expense of children's interests.

Conclusion: A Call to Creative Conflict

In our belief, the public inquiry in Cleveland, whilst endeavouring to adopt the 'rescue' position (Hawkins and Shohet 1989, see Chapter 1) whereby no individuals would be singled out for blame, provided a means for almost everyone to avoid the key issue that here was a way of bringing sexual abuse to light. To some extent the brief given to the inquiry, looking into the arrangements for case management, inevitably resulted in a focus on the key professionals involved. Since the identity of individual children had to be safeguarded throughout, the inquiry withdrew into private session whenever a case was examined in detail. Lay people and most professionals had no opportunity of learning from case material. This consideration, among others, may have led the emphasis away from the central issue – that a way had been found to identify abused children which could break the secrecy surrounding sexual abuse. Keeping the children in focus throughout would also have entailed the provision of extensive resources to meet their needs. It is significant that the two paediatricians were formally reprimanded by the Regional Health Authority for continuing to diagnose when resources were not available. Avoiding the key issues depended on a process of stifling public debate and diverting attention away from thechildren and their needs as represented by their professional advocates.

The Official Solicitor's section of the report (Butler- Sloss, 1988 pp.25–35) which does focus on the children, is probably the least quoted. We believe that in the wake of Cleveland, significantly more professionals are endeavouring to protect children but within a framework of adult consensus, fewer are willing to commit themselves to the role of advocate and carry the children's messages. We relate this to an awareness of the inevitability of conflict which places the individual in a beleaguered position in relation to his peers. The reality is summed up by Bentovim (1988 p.139):

> 'The professional who speaks for the child who has been hurt, can also expect that the 'family' of professionals may well also trivialize, disbelieve, attribute false meanings or just ignore the implication of what has been stated or perceived, and even make the professional who has spoken to the child doubt what he has been told.'

Wells (1990, p.48) comments on the way that many practitioners 'feel victimized by the fact of their advocacy and witness for children' and on how support is needed from 'others who will not deny the existence of such repeated suffering'. We have learned that without the support and understanding of our community we cannot help abused children or create the resources to do so. The size of the problem is potentially so large that professional endeavour alone can never be enough. The task needs to be placed in the context of wider change in attitudes affecting children, which can only come about by a more general 'social healing' (Bagley and King 1990 p. 209). We therefore have to address the task of political change, the nature of which will alter the power imbalance and end the process of exploitation of children by adults and of women by men. As part of this task we need to raise public awareness and create a new alliance between professionals and the wider community on which an active response can be based. This is likely to unbalance existing systems of professional and political control until a new balance of power has been created in which child advocacy will be recognized as the norm.

32

3 The Medical Diagnosis of Child Sexual Abuse: The Paediatrician's Dilemma

Geoff Wyatt and Marietta Higgs

You will readily admit that it would be a good thing to have a second method of arriving at the aetiology of hysteria, one in which we should feel less dependent on the assertions of the patients themselves. A dermatologist, for instance, is able to recognise a sore as leuetic (i.e.syphilitic) from the character of its margins, of the crust on it and of its shape, without being misled by the protestation of his patient, who denies any source of infection for it; and a forensic physician can arrive at the cause of an injury, even if he has to do without any information from the injured person. (Freud, 1886)

Introduction

This chapter describes the 157 children whose details were submitted by us, as two consultant paediatricians, to the Cleveland Inquiry in 1987. The children form two groups. In Group A, there was a concern about sexual abuse before the child saw the paediatrician. In Group B the paediatrician was the first to raise the possibility of sexual abuse in children referred with other health problems. Essential data is provided to show how the medical diagnosis was made for each group. The case for doctors making a medical diagnosis of child sexual abuse is considered together with the factors which influence whether the medical diagnosis is corroborated by a disclosure from the child. The importance of medical intervention especially for children in Group B, who depend on a doctor to initiate the multidisciplinary assessment, will be discussed together with the dilemmas that this creates.

33

The Case For A Medical Diagnosis Of Child Sexual Abuse.

Since doctors usually work in a surgery or hospital clinic, the diagnosis will be made following a process of history taking and examining the child. Paediatricians see children as their patients and are therefore bound to come into contact with child sexual abuse. Some of these children may have symptoms and signs and if they have not disclosed the abuse they depend on a doctor to initiate concern about it. Both doctors and children will benefit from medical practice that accepts and recognises a level of medical concern expressed in terms of 'reasonable medical certainty' (Krugman 1989).

A medical diagnosis of child sexual abuse can be a reference point which can enable other agencies to make a more informed response during a multidisciplinary assessment. This is particularly important in preventative health terms for the young child where the doctor is able to initiate concern (Group B) and may have a vital role in beginning further assessment by making a medical diagnosis. Doctors are more likely to take on this initial responsibility on behalf of children if they believe that an accurate diagnosis is possible and, that in the absence of information to corroborate the diagnosis, they will be supported and protected. Appleyard (1990 p.42) makes the point that:

> If the necessarily strict criteria, that of beyond reasonable doubt, which is required by a criminal court of law are relied upon as the only indicator that child sexual abuse has occurred, then most sexual abuse would remain unrecognised.

To be able to discharge their role in sexual abuse effectively doctors may need first to overcome a sense of hopelessness towards their patients whose health may be suffering because of sexual abuse. The following comments by the British Paediatric Association (Forfar 1988 p.16) show how similar feelings about childhood illness have been overcome by doctors in the past:

> Cancer is the main disease preoccupation of our age, and is no longer a forbidden word. Many remember the darkness which surrounded discussion of the disease in children in the 1930s. When the diagnosis was made there was little further the physicians could do. Then in 1942 came the bizarre news from the U.S.A. that nitrogen mustard, a product developed in the First World War as a lethal gas, was effective against

certain types of cancer of the lymph glands known as lymphoma and lymphosarcoma. However, problems continued:

The next decade (1950s) was a distressing time for children, parents and paediatricians as the latter struggled to discover the effective dosage and necessary duration of treatment with these new drugs. The ulceration of the mouth, the loss of hair, and the wretchedness of the child, which were the unfortunate concommittants of treatment with these drugs, could only be endured. Yet parents, however distressed, never asked for the treatment to be stopped; they realised that they and the paediatrician were held together by a common bond of suffering and hope.

Co-ordinated efforts between professionals from different disciplines, and support from the general public, have resulted in a better outlook for children suffering from childhood illnesses such as cancer. In child abuse generally and in sexual abuse particularly the doctor and the parents must find that common bond of suffering and hope despite all the difficulties that arise.

It may not always be helpful to look on child sexual abuse as a disease process in the organic sense. Nevertheless the health of the child is likely to be at risk in both the short and the longer term. Browne (1986) describes the initial and longterm effects of sexual abuse. Initial effects include fear, anger, hostility, guilt, shame, depression, sleep and eating disturbance, teenage pregnancy, disturbance of sexual behaviour, difficulties at school, truancy, running away from home, early marriage and delinquency. Long term effects include depression, self destructive behaviour, anxiety, feelings of isolation and stigma, poor self esteem, a tendency towards revictimisation, substance abuse, difficulty in trusting others and sexual maladjustment. We agree with Corwin (1988) that short of preventing the sexual victimisation of children, early identification, protection and treatment offer the greatest hope for diminishing its lasting effects.

Whilst doctors sometimes treat their patients symptomatically, they always have to bear in mind that there might be a serious underlying cause. If a patient presents with fever and cough these symptoms can be treated independently but if the underlying cause is an infection e.g. pneumonia, specific treatment is necessary to restore health. Similarly, if a child has symptoms such as soiling, behaviour disturbance and urinary symptoms, each of these may be treated symptomatically but if the cause is sexual abuse further action is necessary to restore health. In any opinion that a doctor gives there is always a spectrum of certainty or uncertainty. When a doctor is certain about his or her opinion a medical diagnosis can be made. When there is uncertainty in the mind of the doctor a medical diagnosis should not be made. The International Collaborative Committee For Child Health (1988) recommends that if gross signs are seen the diagnosis may be made there and then. They cite as an example a child seen, in a routine outpatient clinic, because of soiling.

The doctor's professional obligation to help the child is broadened when other professionals are also looking to the doctor for help. Kerns (1989 p. 177) describes this process:

> With the explosive rise in the reporting of suspected child sexual abuse over the past decade, the socio-legal system has increasingly looked to the medical profession for diagnostic assistance. Given the mismatch of the complexities of a developing child's communication with the traditional evidential requirements of the legal system, and given the heated arena of adversary proceedings, media scrutiny, and passionate lobbies for all parties, it is not surprising that social workers, police officers, lawyers, and judges have turned to medical examiners in pursuit of 'certainty' in alleged child sexual abuse cases. In response, ever increasing numbers of clinicians have been evaluating these children, measuring their findings in the context of their experiential knowledge base of anatomy acquired in paediatrics and gynaecology.

It is important to remember that sexually abused children may have no physical signs on medical examination. Thus on the one hand, a child with no symptoms or signs may disclose abuse to a social worker and name a perpetrator who confesses to a police officer. In that situation there would have been no medical diagnosis but the probable conclusion of both multidisciplinary assessment and court hearing would be that abuse had taken place. On the other hand a doctor may make a medical diagnosis of sexual abuse on the basis of symptoms and signs. There may be no corroborative information and this may result in the case not going to court. Nevertheless, the doctor should be able to say on behalf of the child that there is a medical diagnosis of sexual abuse. In other cases, on the basis of the symptoms and signs, the doctor may reach the opinion that sexual abuse is a differential diagnosis but that opinion will fall short of the degree of certainty required to make a medical diagnosis. In this way there would still be flexibility for doctors accurately to express their opinion. If the multidisciplinary framework is strong it should be able to accommodate the full spectrum of medical opinion. This would decrease the risk of scapegoating individual professionals when difficulties arise.

It is recognised that, as in any other subject, the knowledge base will change in the future. Nevertheless the process of multidisciplinary assessment involves attributing the appropriate weight to any level of medical concern expressed by the doctor. The responsibility for making the medical diagnosis rests solely with the doctor. If this is the only information which has come to light as a result of the assessment, the doctor is dependent on the multidisciplinary framework to avoid becoming isolated and vulnerable to criticism and discreditation. There are two possible responses in this situation: one is for the doctor to avoid making a medical diagnosis at all: the other is to use the medical information to alert the system without giving a medical diagnosis. As doctors we regard both of these options as unacceptable. We have to accept the risk that a medical diagnosis may sometimes not be corroborated, with the result that the doctor may be discredited.

Presentation and the Importance of the Child's History

Before 1987, medical involvement in child sexual abuse was usually confined to Group A children. The police evidence to the inquiry describes a change in the way the police came to be involved. This historical shift in context is tellingly outlined in the Cleveland report:

They (the police) were accustomed to receiving referrals for involvement in the investigation of sexual offences by complaint from the victim either directly or through a third party or agency such as parent, social worker, health visitor, school etc. This was called by Mr. White the 'traditional route'. The reports now coming to them were from non-traditional routes:

1. They originated from the examination of the child at hospital by a paediatrician:
2. In some cases the referral to the paediatrician appeared to be unconnected with sexual abuse:
3. In some cases the child was of such tender years that any complaint or disclosure by the child was unlikely to be obtained in the conventional manner.(Butler-Sloss 1988 p.93)

A paper by Hobbs and Wynne (1986) drew attention to the importance of taking a thorough history and to certain techniques in the medical examination. Roberts (1986) countered 'Without a more thorough investigation it is not possible even to be sure what is being alleged'. Hobbs and Wynne (1986,) responded that their patients differed from those seen by Roberts in several respects; they were younger, there were more boys and the presentation was more varied. Hobbs and Wynne (1987 p.837-841) reviewed 337 referrals in 1985-86:

39% presented because they had disclosed abuse, 11% presented after allegation by relative or carer; 16% were siblings or children in contact with a suspected or proven abuser, 10% presented with physical abuse. In 22% alerting symptoms or indicators led to referral- including behavioral (7%), nonspecific physical or psychosomatic (3%), and genital or anal (12%) signs and symptoms. 2% were detected during routine examination in special schools.

The paediatricians and police surgeons in Cleveland in 1987 were to experience similar differences in their acceptance of the observations of Drs. Hobbs and Wynne. (Butler-Sloss, 1988 p.14).

In Cleveland, out of the 157 children , 82 were referred directly to the paediatricians (index children). The paediatricians asked to see 75 because they were either a sibling or a close associate of an index child. It is normal practice in child abuse work to assess the siblings and associates of index children. Out of the 82 index children (i.e. those referred directly to the paediatrician), 42 belonged to Group A and 40 to Group B. (see introduction) Allegations were made that Group B children who attended hospital for routine injuries and ailments were subjected to examination for sexual abuse (Butler-Sloss, 1988 p. 164) This was rejected by the inquiry report:

> The inquiry was satisfied from the evidence presented that there was no routine screening for sexual abuse. In each instance of a child attending hospital for 'routine injuries and ailments' there were grounds in the professional judgement of the examining consultant for the investigation of the child for the possibility of sexual abuse (Butler-Sloss, 1988 p.165).

Because the children in Group B did not present in the traditional manner, physical signs, in particular reflex anal dilatation became the subject of intense debate in both the lay and professional press. Hobbs and Wynne (1987) subsequently reported an increasing rate of diagnosis in child sexual abuse and further correspondence followed in the Lancet (1987 Oct.31p.1017, Nov.21p.1217, Dec.12 p.1396) about whether reflex anal dilatation was indicative of child sexual abuse. Just before the Cleveland report was published, reflex anal dilatation was associated with bowel disease. (Evans and Walker Smith; Magnay and Insley 1988). Butler–Sloss (1988, p.193) concluded from the evidence that 'the consensus is that the sign of anal dilatation is abnormal and suspicious and requires further investigation. It is not in itself evidence of anal abuse'. The report also addressed the concern that the diagnosis was based solely upon this sign, but stated that 'in only 18 cases out of 121 cases was it the sole physical sign and in no case was it the sole ground for the diagnosis' (Butler–Sloss, 1988 p.165). On the basis of our usual medical practice in other clinical situations namely by interpretation of the history and examination, we felt able to make a medical diagnosis in 121 children out of the 157 seen.

The 36 remaining children did not have physical signs (see later) to enable a medical diagnosis to be made. Krugman (1989) states:

The medical diagnosis of sexual abuse usually cannot be made on the basis of physical findings alone. With the exception of acquired gonorrhoea or syphilis, or the presence of forensic evidence of sperm or semen, there are no pathognomonic findings for sexual abuse. Critical to this diagnosis is a child's history. A hymenal diameter of more than 4 mm alone, reflex anal dilatation alone, or a scar at six o clock alone is not diagnostic of sexual abuse. Observing these findings should make one want to know more, and should lead to a multidisciplinary investigation if the history is positive. Courts can then decide whether there is enough information available to reach a level of certainty to enable to civilly protect a child, and/or enough to permit the criminal prosecution.

Guidance For Doctors (DHSS 1988) also emphasises the history of the child's complaint or health problem and advises doctors that 'child sexual abuse should be remembered in the differential diagnosis of many physical conditions'. Appleyard (1990 p.43) in support of Guidance For Doctors (DHSS 1988) goes on to say: 'No one physical symptom or sign is absolutely diagnostic of child sexual abuse. However, patterns of symptoms and signs may be diagnostic'.

We think that the child's medical history can directly suggest the possibility of child sexual abuse (Group A) or indirectly by way of symptoms of illness (Group B). If on examination, the paediatrician then finds physical signs consistent with child sexual abuse, a medical diagnosis of sexual abuse could be made. This medical diagnosis is the doctor's contribution and does not replace or anticipate the 'overall diagnosis' which results from the multidisciplinary assessment. Unless a medical diagnosis is made, children in Group B may not benefit from a multidisciplinary assessment. Doctors can and should take responsibility for identifying the possibility of abuse in these children with health problems. Unless doctors refer these children on for further assessment their health problem may persist.

Cleveland's Children: Essential Data.

During a seven month period in 1987 there were 2708 attendances at the paediatric outpatients, Middlesbrough General Hospital. 157 children who were presented to the Cleveland Inquiry were mainly seen in May and June. Figure 3.1 shows how these children were classified.

Figure 3.1a

THE MEDICAL DIAGNOSIS OF SEXUAL ABUSE IN INDEX CHILDREN AND IN SIBLINGS OR ASSOCIATES.

	Index children.	Siblings or associates.	All children.
TOTAL	82	75	157
Medical diagnosis of sexual abuse.	74 (90%)	47 (63%)	121 (77%)
No medical diagnosis.	8 (10%)	28 (37%)	36 (23%)

Figure 3.1b.

MEDICAL DIAGNOSIS OF SEXUAL ABUSE IN GROUP A
AND GROUP B CHILDREN.

| | Group A | | | Group B | | |
	Index.	Sibling/ assoc.	All Gp. A.	Index.	Sibling/ assoc.	All Gp.B.
TOTAL	42	16	58	40	59	99
Medical diagnosis of sexual abuse.	35 (83%)	7 (44%)	42 (72%)	39 (98%)	40 (68%)	79 (80%)
No medical diagnosis of sexual abuse.	7 (17%)	9 (56%)	16 (28%)	1 (2%)	19 (32%)	20 (20%)

Group A: Index children were referred to the paediatrician with an existing concern of sexual abuse. Group B: Index children were referred to the paediatrician with a health problem but no pre-existing concern of sexual abuse. Group A and Group B siblings and associates were requested to attend because of concerns of sexual abuse in index children. The 157 children are those where a high level of concern existed. In 121 children the doctor expressed a medical diagnosis of sexual abuse and in 36 children a medical diagnosis was not made. In other words we believed no other cause could explain the symptoms and signs in 121 children. Of the remaining 36 children, there was a pre-existing concern of sexual abuse in 35 of them (7 index Group A, 28 sibling associates) and in one index child in Group B there was a concern of physical abuse; however there were insufficient physical signs to make a medical diagnosis of sexual abuse.

There was another group of children not included here and not reviewed by the inquiry, where the medical diagnosis was considered but not made because the doctor was unsure. In these children there were symptoms leading to referral to a paediatrician so they were potentially

Group B children. In these circumstances a doctor is dependent upon the presence of physical signs to make a medical diagnosis.

Returning to the 157 children considered by the Inquiry, there were more siblings and associate children in Group B (59) than in Group A (16). This is because children with a health problem (Group B) are usually referred and seen individually, whereas when a concern about sexual abuse is raised e.g. by a social worker (Group A), the siblings and associates of that child may all be referred to the paediatrician as index children.

The mode of referral and reason for referral in Group A and Group B children differ as shown in figures 3.2 and 3.3.

Figure 3.2.

MODE OF REFERRAL.	GROUP A	GROUP B
Social Services.	32	2
Outpatient revisit.	2	20
General Practitioner.	3	8
Hospital doctors and nurses.	0	7
Community doctors and nurses.	3	3
Guardian ad litem.	1	0
Parent.	1	0
TOTAL.	42	40

Figure 3.3

REASON FOR REFERRAL: GROUP A. GROUP B.

	GROUP A	GROUP B
Concern re. sexual abuse.	37	0
Previous child abuse.	0	1
Nonaccidental injury.	0	8
Concern re. child care.	1	2
Behaviour problem.	3	5
Growth problem.	0	4
Developmental problem.	0	2
Urinary problem.	0	4
Vaginal problem.	1	4
Anal problem.	0	10
TOTAL:	42	40

Guidance for Doctors (DHSS 1988), asks doctors to remember the possibility of sexual abuse in certain physical conditions: non-accidental injury; lower genitourinary tract symptoms, injuries and abnormalities; faecal soiling, retention or rectal bleeding; rectal abnormalities and sexually transmitted disease. The guidance also mentions behavioural and emotional problems. 80 percent of the index children in Group B had one of these physical or behavioural conditions. An additional factor influencing the doctor's opinion is the length of time that the patient has been suffering from the symptoms. Sadly, half of the children in Group B had had symptoms for longer than a year and fifteen of them for over two years.

Butler-Sloss (1988 p194) cites other clinical situations for example, failure to thrive, where a thorough examination including the ano-genital region is recommended. In addition Appendix B (Butler-Sloss 1988 p.277) includes wider criteria quoted by the Tavistock Foundation (1984): other physical indicators (both anogenital and general) and behavioural (sexual and general). All the children in Group B would be encompassed in these criteria, either as having some indicator of sexual abuse or, on the basis of the history, the need for a complete physical examination.

Most Group B children had already been seen by doctors on previous occasions without child sexual abuse being considered. One half of them were estimated to have received over three hours of medical consideration as outpatients, inpatients or in follow up appointments. Despite this no explanation had been found for their continuing problems.

A medical diagnosis of sexual abuse was made for 35 out of the 42 Group A children. In the 7 remaining children there were no findings on physical examination and no medical diagnosis was made. This does not disprove sexual abuse since the abuse may not have left physical signs, or the signs may have resolved. In Group B the symptoms and signs were sufficient for a medical diagnosis of child sexual abuse to be made for 39 out of the 40 children. It cannot be emphasised too strongly that the medical diagnosis is based on both symptoms and signs.

The physical signs present for children in each group are shown in the figure 3.4.

Figure 3.4

PHYSICAL SIGNS.	GROUP A	GROUP B.
On or below 3rd percentile wt. or wt. and ht.	7	11
Bruising consistent with nonaccidental injury.	6	14
Anal skin verge.abnormality.	14	25
Reflex relaxation of anal sphincter.	29	35
Dilatation of the anal orifice.	26	35

Figure 3.4 (cont.)

PHYSICAL SIGNS.	GROUP A	GROUP B.
Fissuring or fissures.	18	24
Abnormal genitalia.	22	19
Number of children with a medical diagnosis	35	39

Two index children in Group A, and one index child in Group B had only one physical sign: reflex anal dilatation. The Group B child also had one of the health problems quoted in the Guidance for Doctors(DHSS 1988)

The Independent Panel.

Further information on the accuracy of the diagnosis in Cleveland is available from the conclusions of an independent panel of consultants. This was set up by the Northern Regional Health Authority at the request of Cleveland social services to provide second opinions on children where the diagnosis was disputed. (Butler-Sloss, 1988, p.117) The panel elected to review only those children where parental consent was forthcoming so that their sample was highly selective. They saw 29 children from 12 families; 8 of these families were already known to social services. In 86 percent of the children the independent panel agreed with the diagnoses or the concern of the doctors. The diagnosis was confirmed in 12 children and in another 6 the signs were considered sufficient to warrant further investigations. In 7 children the panel supported the original medical opinion that there were no findings indicative of abuse. In four children the original diagnosis of abuse was not confirmed. However, it is important to remember that time had elapsed between the original opinion and the second examination. (Butler-Sloss, 1988, p.118.)

Corroboration of the Medical Diagnosis: Pointers from the Cleveland Children

The age of the child is a factor in whether the medical diagnosis will be corroborated by a disclosure. 45 of the total of 121 children with a medical diagnosis of child sexual abuse made a disclosure. The mean age of these 45 children was 7.43 years (Standard Deviation = 3.03 years). The 76 children who did not make a disclosure can be divided into two groups, 33 for whom there was supportive information of child sexual abuse, and 43 for whom there was none. The 33 children who had supportive information but did not make a disclosure were considerably younger, with a mean age of 5.86 years (Standard Deviation=3.08 years). For these 33 children, supportive information included sexual behaviour/abuse observed, worrying comments made, previous non-accidental injury or suspected sexual abuse, and behavioural symptoms. The 43 children who did not disclose and had no supportive information were even younger, with a mean age of 4.57 years (Standard Deviation = 3.22 years.) The youngest child in this group was under one year.

The availability of a safe, neutral environment also influenced whether the child disclosed. Of the 45 children who made a disclosure of a sexual nature, 36 did not do so until admitted to hospital or foster care. Of the 9 other children able to disclose without the safe environment 8 disclosed abuse by a perpetrator who was not living with the child at the time.

These figures are consistent with those for an overlapping but largely separate group of children evaluated by the clinical psychologist over the same period. Of the 40 children referred with suspected sexual abuse or a medical diagnosis of sexual abuse, 21 had medical findings and 16 of these 21 children subsequently disclosed abuse by a named perpetrator. Three prepubertal girls with both anal and vaginal findings vehemently denied that anything had happened, and a boy and girl, both of two years, were unable to say anything. A total of 32 children out of the whole group of 40 made a disclosure, 8 of them prior to the assessment and medical examination. Only one of these 8 children disclosed while still living at home with the named abuser. The timing of the disclosure for the remaining children varied. 9 of the remaining 32 disclosed during or immediately after the medical examination but 13 of them did not speak until the psychological assessment had taken place. In some cases this was months afterwards. There may not have been sufficient time for some of the diagnosed children to reach the point of readiness to disclose (Chapter 5) before investigation finished or was terminated by legal proceedings and the children returned home.

A sensitive medical interview and examination may help a child towards disclosure. Children are unlikely to say anything spontaneously during a medical consultation, but it is part of normal medical practice to ask for clarification if something is found on examination, especially in the case of children wheremost if not all of the history has been given by a third party. For example the doctor may find a lump which the child has not previously mentioned to anyone and may need more information: how long it has been there, whether it comes and goes and so on. The doctor will ask the child, if he or she is old enough. With some of the children in Cleveland, a neutral comment such as 'it looks as though something has been happening to your bottom' was sometimes responded to by a disclosure of abuse.

Concern was raised in another way when a social worker noted that the father of a group A child was on record as a schedule 1 offender previously convicted of indecent assault on young boys. He had received no treatment. The subsequent case conference requested a medical examination and the 11 year old girl was found to have signs consistent with anal abuse. During the medical consultation the doctor had said, 'it looks as though something might have been happening to you down here'. Afterwards in the police/social work interview the child readily described anal abuse.

Some children may be too young or too frightened or loyal to the abuser to respond to this approach. For example, a group B girl of 7 years had been referred to the paediatric outpatients by the school doctor who was concerned about her poor growth. There were no obvious medical reasons to account for this. During the history taking, episodes of great unhappiness were described for which she had given no reason. After physical examination it was put to her that it looked as though something had been happening to her bottom and her front. She dropped her head and eyes and nodded. It took her months, while living with a foster family, to be able to tell of regular abuse by her uncle. Both Group A and B children depend on trusting adults, in many cases the doctor, to take the responsibility for speaking on their behalf. Since 1987 many adults who were abused during childhood have found the strength to speak out. Many describe how as children they saw various doctors with a variety of non-specific problems for which no explanation was given. They would sometimes deliberately feign illness such as abdominal pain. They had thought and hoped that somehow the doctor would see what was happening and help them.

To summarise, the likelihood of obtaining a corroborative disclosure for a medical diagnosis of child sexual abuse often depends on the child's age and the safety of his or her environment during the multidisciplinary assessment. The absence of a disclosure does not necessarily mean that the diagnosis is incorrect, it simply means that there is no corroboration. Young children will be disadvantaged if the criterion for beginning a multidisciplinary assessment is a disclosure by the child rather than a medical diagnosis of sexual abuse. In other areas of preventative medicine, for example, immunisation, developmental assessment and the identification of rare metabolic diseases, society concentrates its resources on young children. Child sexual abuse should be no exception to this. Lafontaine (1990) says:

> What abused children most want, according to survivors,sounds relatively simple to provide: they want to be believed, they want information and they want help to stop the abuse.

Dilemmas for the Doctor.

Guidance for Doctors (DHSS 1988) stops short of advising doctors when they should make a medical diagnosis of sexual abuse. This may leave doctors uncertain as to when they should initiate concern for a child with a health problem. Further difficulty arises from misunderstanding about whether a medical diagnosis can ever prove anything in a legal sense. Although it is rare in medicine to find uniquely diagnostic signs for any condition, differences in medical opinion which fuel the adversarial nature of court proceedings arise from the expectation that doctors can be relied upon to prove whether abuse has occurred.

The Butler-Sloss Report is ambivalent about the term medical diagnosis. Whilst stating that child sexual abuse 'is the cause of the child's symptoms and signs and in that limited sense child sexual abuse is the diagnosis of the child's problem' the report also states that 'child sexual abuse describes aberrant adult behaviour; it causes physical and emotional damage to the child'. Doctors may be left confused by the conclusion: 'while recognising that it is not an accurate description, the term 'diagnosis' has been used throughout the course of the Inquiry to describe the conclusion reached from the symptoms and signs'. (Butler-Sloss,1988 p.183). At the same time many people may have unresolved doubts about whether the children diagnosed in Cleveland were sexually abused. Butler-Sloss (1988,p.183) explicitly states 'It is not the function of the inquiry to evaluate the accuracy of any diagnosis nor to resolve conflicting evidence nor to assess whether an individual child was or was not sexually abused'.

One dilemma is that if the doctor waits until the child has come forward with an alerting statement, the responsibility for bringing the abuse to light then remains with the child, who may never be able to speak. Taken to the extreme, and seen in the context of other medical problems, the doctor would have to seek confirmation of the medical diagnosis only in the post mortem room. If the doctor decides not to make a medical diagnosis he carries the responsibility for leaving the child unprotected and at continued risk of ill health which may continue into adult life. The key dilemma for the doctor, however, is that if he raises a cause for concern about sexual abuse in a child where there is no prior complaint and where the medical diagnosis is not supported by the subsequent assessment, he may be accused of starting a process of secondary abuse. For example, if a child is removed from the home only to be returned months later because a court felt there was insufficient medical evidence to prove that sexual abuse had occurred, the doctor may be blamed for the trauma inflicted on the child and family.

We have described factors which affect corroboration of the medical diagnosis by a disclosure. A rational approach to resolving the doctor's dilemma depends on a balanced assessment of these factors. Doctors need to be supported by other professionals and society generally so that they can raise concern when appropriate. A multidisciplinary approach can then help both the child and others involved in the abuse, particularly the perpetrator and the family. When the doctor is the first to raise concern the opinion given must be as accurate and helpful as the current knowledge allows. The crucial question for doctors is what they may consider to be adequate to initiate concern and how to work with other professionals to respond creatively on behalf of the child.

Conclusion: Professional and Political Considerations.

There have always been professional and political implications for doctors who highlight issues that society finds unpalatable. Gaulter (1833) describes the scene following a medical diagnosis of cholera at a time when there was little therapy and commonly a fatal outcome: 'Here the scene which followed the announcement of the van [for removing corpses] was often most distressing. While the neighbours insist on removal, the relations would refuse to allow it and support their refusal by a denial of the nature of the disease'. Over 150 years later in Cleveland the unacceptability of sexual abuse may have led to a similar denial.

We believe that some of the public furore which accompanied the crisis was essentially a reaction to child sexual abuse becoming visible. The inquiry focused on the professionals involved, but the uncertainty as to what the interaction between the doctor and the child can include remains unresolved. There must be an ongoing debate about the role of the paediatrician in identifying children who may have been sexually abused. It is vital that paediatricians are able to exercise their professional judgement and that they are free from political restraint. Society must advance beyond crisis rather than retreat from it.

The General Medical Council, the British Medical Association and the Defence Organisations all support the view that it is the duty of the doctor to initiate concern for some children. (DHSS 1988). The bleak alternative for Group B children is that doctors may choose only to respond to concerns raised about child sexual abuse by other professionals and so concern themselves with Group A children only. Since the publication of the inquiry report and Guidance for Doctors there has been a significant drop in the numbers of children referred from Middlesbrough General Hospital to the social services by the paediatricians. In 1987 there were 76 such referrals, in 1989 there were only four children referred for joint examination by paediatricians.

Whilst the focus of the medical diagnosis is the child's health, the multidisciplinary assessment must have regard for possible legal proceedings. Doctors need to be willing and able to justify their diagnosis so that other people, professionals and the lay community can understand how and why they come to that view. The next chapter deals with problems and issues of management which follow from the medical diagnosis.

4 After the Medical Diagnosis: Everyone's Dilemma

Geoff Wyatt and Marietta Higgs

One point which has not really emerged from the report is that children are now being recognised as probably abused before they 'have disclosed' ie. they are not ready. In the past 'disclosure' or an allegation to the police was the usual presentation of child sexual abuse. We know many children never describe their abuse, others only after months in the safety of a foster home. Children left at home may be threatened and never feel able to disclose, and without some sort of admission from them, child professionals are increasingly anxious about taking any action. Yet it may be only by removal of the child from the abuser that the child can develop the confidence to tell. (Wynne, 1988)

Introduction

This chapter considers how the medical opinion becomes part of the wider assessment, particularly when the doctor raises the initial concern about sexual abuse. In all aspects of paediatric practice parents are involved because they are responsible for the care of their children. This parental responsibility has to be addressed by the multidisciplinary team in the management of suspected child sexual abuse. A model is suggested for investigation depending on whether the child is in Group A or Group B

Immediately After the Medical Diagnosis; The Cleveland Experience.

Once a medical diagnosis has been made other people need to become involved, since doctors have a duty to report sexual abuse. Guidance for Doctors (DHSS 1988) in essence endorses medical practice in Cleveland in 1987. The inquiry (Butler-Sloss,1988, p.250) recognised identification by a paediatrician of possible abuse as a referral route although the subsequent management is not advised in detail. The multidisciplinary assessment may then begin without any disclosure by the child. Effective assessment therefore depends on the willingness of other professionals to accept the medical diagnosis as one piece of the jigsaw.

The process of gathering the information may take time. It may depend on the age of the child and the availability of a safe neutral environment (Chapters 3 and 6). Particular difficulties may arise when, as is always the case with Group B and sometimes with Group A, the abuser is unknown. From the evidence available (Finkelhor, 1986, Bentovim 1988) as the majority of abusers are known to the child and may be living in the same household, the abuser may silence the child. Other family pressures may hinder disclosure and further inquiries by professionals may be fruitless. In this situation, the doctor is not simply dealing with the child as a patient, but with a complex series of processes within the child, the family and society as a whole. Admission to hospital can help to protect the child and provide appropriate space for all parties in the initial stages of investigation. In the early stages of our management of children where child sexual abuse was suspected following the medical diagnosis, the child admitted to hospital, often was accompanied by the mother. This avoided separating the child completely from its family but provided support for the child and other family members and some control over access. In co-operation with the social services department, at specific stages of the investigation, parents were sometimes requested not to visit or to do so only under certain conditions. This was regarded as good practice in respect of children who had not yet disclosed or who were in the early stages of disclosure. In the first instance, many of the admissions to hospital were with the agreement of the parents. Figures 4.1 and 4.2 give details of their subsequent placement and access arrangements.

Following the medical diagnosis it was practice in Cleveland to examine the siblings (or associates in the case of children who were fostered or minded daily). In some instances, sibling groups were also admitted to the wards. Sometimes corroborative information was obtained from siblings, which was especially useful for some index children who were too young to disclose on their own behalf. Although similar practice was already established and accepted with physical abuse, in the case of child sexual abuse it proved highly controversial and the debate about its helpfulness has been obscured by the public and media outcry focusing on the separation of families. The need for an environment in which children feel safe to disclose sexual abuse cannot be overstated. It is important to retain what the hospital can offer as part of a flexible series of options for the child, especially in respect of children who can thus be enabled to move to the point of disclosure. (Ch. 5).

Figure 4.1

Placement of Children Following the Medical Diagnosis.

Returned to previous residence.	10
Returned to previous residence after hospital admission.	26
Immediate foster home.	17 ⋆
Foster home after hospital admission.	68
Total number of children.	121

⋆ The children who went straight to foster homes from the paediatric outpatients were either in Group A or there were prior concerns about physical abuse.

Figure 4.2

Visiting Arrangements For Those Children Admitted To Hospital.

Resident parent or open visiting	86
Restricted or no parental access	8
Total number of children admitted	94

As more children were diagnosed services became overloaded and it was difficult to provide parents and children with support on the wards. This situation is commonly faced by doctors, for instance during epidemics, when the usual practice would be that the doctor will trawl all available resources for the benefit of the patient. During the Cleveland 'Crisis', a resource centre was set up jointly by the District Health Authority and the local authority to provide a child-centered environment within the hospital, support for families and facilities for professionals to investigate as a multidisciplinary team. Since the Child Resource Centre was in the grounds of Middlesbrough General Hospital, medical practice could be adapted as part of a multidisciplinary protocol whereby parents were not necessarily told of the medical diagnosis before other agencies had been alerted and a strategy formulated. However, any protocol which alters existing patterns of professional behaviour has the potential to alert or alarm the family. In other words, a decision not to inform parents before the multidisciplinary team has met can itself prompt reactions of suspicion, anxiety or hostility. The doctor could then easily be isolated and divorced from the framework of normal medical practice, and by failing to meet the usual expectations of parents when they bring their children to see a doctor, may threaten the child's health.

The dilemma encountered within the consulting room with child and parent when a medical diagnosis of child sexual abuse is made cannot be easily resolved by establishing interdisciplinary procedures, since these cannot alter public perceptions of established medical practice i.e. expectations of how the doctor will behave in any medical consultation. Open debate is needed so that the principle of child health can be seen as integral to the management of child sexual abuse. In response to inter-agency conflict in Cleveland a decision was taken by the social services department to admit children to hospital on a place of safety order, signed by a magistrate. Like admission to hospital, this practice was intended to facilitate investigation and disclosure. We believe this step was necessary because the medical diagnosis was disputed.

Another conflict can arise in the consulting room because child sexual abuse is a criminal act and evidential requirements must be addressed. During the medical consultation the child may not have said anything spontaneously about abuse. Does the doctor gently probe or should the questioning be left to the people designated to carry out a formal interview i.e. police officer and social worker. The needs of the child and the professionals may not coincide; the doctor may feel vulnerable in the absence of corroborative information whilst the child may not feel safe enough to disclose.

Involving the Parents in Multidisciplinary Assessment.

Doctor and parents usually form a partnership where the common aim is the child's welfare. A doctor would expect the relationship with patient or parents to continue until the presenting problem is resolved. Parents usually expect an opinion from the doctor, and the way in which this is given will influence the future relationship between doctor and family. This in turn will influence whether for example medications are taken, and whether the patient or parent can be totally honest and open about their problems and concerns. Doctors usually achieve this with other childhood health problems by being open and honest with parents. The Inquiry Report recommends (Butler-Sloss, 1988 p.246) 'Parents should be informed and where appropriate consulted at each stage of the investigation by the professional dealing with the child, whether medical, police or social worker. Parents are entitled to know what is going on, and to be helped to understand the steps that are being taken'. However, the report also comments (p.141) that 'this practice of immediate communication to the parents of a firm and unequivocal diagnosis created difficulties for both social services and the police'. In the context of child abuse, particularly sexual abuse, a dilemma may arise when the doctor has completed his or her consultation as to how much, or what, to say to the parents.

On the one hand, if parents are fully informed at the outset, there is the possibility of mobilising protective forces in the family to remove the risk to the child. This is more likely to be the case for Group A children, where the diagnosis follows from other causes for concern. The parent's response can be difficult to predict. This approach relies on the child being protected from pressures to retract, and on mobilising support for non-abusing carers who can maintain a protective position. On the other hand, complex factors such as the nature of perpetrator behaviour, together with the child's place on the continuum of readiness described in Chapter 5, mean that informing the parents at an early stage may simply serve adult agendas to disbelieve or silence the child, especially for children in Group B. 'In Cleveland we heard of examples of pressure on children. A girl of 12 told the official solicitor that her stepfather said no one would believe her. A girl of 8 expressed relief at the death of her father who committed suicide after she revealed the abuse' (Butler-Sloss, 1988, p.7). Doctors in Cleveland followed their training and kept parents informed; 'Some parents expressed relief and gratitude at the discovery of hitherto unknown sexual abuse of their children from either within or outside the family' (Butler-Sloss, 1988, p.36). As a result, some children were protected by their parents. In other instances the same approach was met with parental hostility. This is an unresolved dilemma for the doctor.

No matter how the initial concern is raised, the success of the multi-disciplinary assessment depends on gathering as much further information as possible from the child, parents, brothers and sisters and sometimes other people concerned with the family. However, it must be remembered that a child has time limits. One view is that investigation should proceed at the child's pace or somehow that if things are done slowly enough this will reduce the upset and trauma which occurs when a diagnosis of child sexual abuse is made. It is difficult to see how this may benefit very young, damaged or disturbed children. The relatively short-lived stage of child-hood is of critical importance for a healthy adult life. Aspects of growth such as physical, emotional, social, intellectual, and moral development are interdependent and may all be affected by abuse of any sort. Besides damage to these developmental tasks there is also the pain, and misery that an abused child has to endure in silence. Knowing this, the doctor, who may well be seeing a child and parents in the outpatient clinic on a Friday afternoon has to decide; 'do I say anything now or do I wait longer?' For some children where the clinical evidence is not very strong or the doctor is uncertain, the appropriate course of action may be to wait longer and review later in the outpatient department. It is accepted that this is a condition which is not usually immediately life-threatening. However delay can prevent validation, especially when the diagnosis is disputed. A large group of children in Cleveland were not reviewed by the inquiry because there were insufficient symptoms or signs for a medical diagnosis. The approach begs the question whether there will ever be more information available to the doctor to enable him to act and if it is, how long the process might take. Meanwhile, the doctor is sending the child home to an unknown situation where any abuse may continue with no other opportunity to bring the concern out into the open. There are gross instances of lost opportunities in inquiries into cases of physically abused children killed following an inadequate response to a window of oppor-tunity.

Sometimes the doctor may decide to voice a concern because there are, on examination, clear physical signs which can be recorded for evidential purposes. This action will also help the child by removing the need for a second examination for further opinion. A clinical photograph may demonstrate the signs. Some physical signs may disappear (Cantwell 1987). Butler-Sloss, (1988, p.247) notes that information on the natural history of physical signs is lacking, for example, in relation to the frequency and type of abuse. If the doctor decides to wait before expressing a concern, the next time the child is seen the signs may no longer be there.

It is clear from programmes developed to treat perpetrators (eg. Roundy and Horton 1990) that without a mandate most perpetrators would not opt to go through the process. However, other family members, such as non-abusing carers and children, may not necessarily need a controlling framework. Without a thorough assessment the details of the problems which would form the basis of a plan to help both child and family are unlikely to be gathered. The multidisciplinary team must also decide whether other professionals involved in the assessment need an opportunity to gather more information -perhaps by talking with the child or others involved with the child – before giving the parents the doctor's information.

We feel that the parents have to be involved and this becomes the first challenge and test of the commitment to multidisciplinary assessment by all the professionals involved. However, we recognise that in some cases this may jeopardise the work with the child. More debate is needed to resolve this crucial issue, which will be raised again in Chapter 8.

Framework for the Multidisciplinary Assessment.

Butler-Sloss (1988, p.249) recommended that Specialist Assessment Teams should be established 'to undertake a full assessment of the child and the family in cases of particular difficulty'. The team was envisaged as offering an assessment but not treatment or a plan for the future, ie. to provide information which can assist in case management/decision-making: 'the completion of a medical examination, social work assessment, and appropriate inquiries by the police, carried out in a planned and co-ordinated way should allow the Specialist Assessment Team to present their joint assessment and conclusions to the referring agency or a case conference' (Butler-Sloss 1988, p.249).

The report gives few details as to the social service or police involvement in such a team other than that they be trained, experienced and competent in the field of child sexual abuse to undertake the work required. More

detail is given for doctors who should have:

> knowledge and experience of the needs of children and an understanding of child abuse in general and child sexual abuse in particular. They should be prepared, at the request of their medical colleagues, social services or the police to examine a child and participate in a formal multidisciplinary assessment of the child's presenting concern. This may include collecting forensic evidence; compiling medical evidence for care proceedings; and involve attendance at case conferences and at Court. The doctors included on such a list might be community or hospital paediatricians, or those who have appropriate experience such as women police doctors, police surgeons etc. (Butler-Sloss, 1988, p.249)

Particular emphasis has been given to the legal contribution. Butler-Sloss suggests (1989, p.158) that if better legal advice had been available from the local authority the medical dissention might have been avoided 'a lawyer might just have said to them'

> " Well if all these doctors cannot agree, why do we not start looking at other evidence and other factors?"

While we accept this, it begs the question of how further information will be obtained, certainly from the child, unless some action has already been taken to make the child safer and to overcome resistance in the family.

The report presents a flow-chart (Butler-Sloss, 1988, p.250)where a framework would allow straightforward cases to be dealt with in a straightforward way. It is not suggested that the specialist team deal with all referrals. Thus the report quite clearly anticipates different levels of investigation for the possibility of sexual abuse. Straightforward cases are described as follows: referrals which present a straightforward pattern of information, clear account by a child, admission by a perpetrator and confirmation by a medical examination (Butler-Sloss, 1988, p.249). A planned intervention to collect evidence is followed by a case conference to make decisions as to criminal or civil proceedings. The combination of primary medical signs and an allegation by the child will allow a definite conclusion to be drawn. If the allegations relate to a person outside the family, the police would normally investigate and prosecute without the involvement of other agencies. Less straightforward cases are described as presenting the possibility of sexual abuse on the basis of physical or behavioural signs alone, or where there is uncertainty as to whether or not abuse has occurred. (Butler-Sloss, 1988, p.251). In our belief this will be the majority of cases as we develop a more sophisticated approach to detection and intervention.

Cleveland Children; Assessment Data.

On the face of it, children in Group A should be more straightforward to assess than those in Group B. However, even in Group A there are points that raise difficulties with the assessment. For example, 3 of the 42 children referred with a pre-existing concern about sexual abuse (Group A) disclosed abuse but because they had no physical signs, there was no corroborative medical diagnosis.

Butler-Sloss (1988 p.251) recommends that children in Group B 'where suspicion is raised by the presence of physical signs without complaint by the child or a third party' should be referred to a Specialist Assessment Team for a multidisciplinary assessment. It is important to stress that children in Group B would not have been examined were it not for the presence of symptoms of illness which led them to be referred to a paediatrician. Understanding sexual abuse as a health problem can create the context for such children to receive help. Figure 4.3 shows the degree to which supportive data was available for children in both groups.

For the more straightforward Group A children, the assessment produced information supportive of the medical diagnosis and existing concern in every case, either directly from the child or from another child associated with them. In the less straightforward cases, Group B, there were 6 children, average age 3.5 years, where there was no supportive information for medical diagnosis. It is difficult to determine whether these children had been sexually abused. A case conference may chose the 'watching brief' (Butler-Sloss, 1988 p.251) option in their management. This group of children will be examined further in Chapters 5 and 6.

Conflicts and Choices for the Doctor in the Multidisciplinary Team.

In practice, the process of multidisciplinary work has complex dynamics and is prone to difficulties (Stephenson 1989). Children in Group B are more likely to be the subject of conflict and disagreement between

Figure 4.3.

	SUPPORTIVE DATA IN GROUP A INDEX CHILDREN WITH A MEDICAL DIAGNOSIS. (total 35)		SUPPORTIVE DATA IN GROUP B INDEX CHILDREN WITH A MEDICAL DIAGNOSIS (total 39)	
	INDEX	SIBLING★	INDEX	SIBLING★
Disclosure	22	4	8	3
Sexualised behaviour	3	0	2	0
Worrying comment	1	1	6	3
Previous child abuse	2	0	3	2
Behaviour problem	2	0	4	2

★ The numbers in the SIBLING column refer to the number of index children who did not have supportive information themselves but did have a sibling with the supportive information shown.

agencies, who have different perceptions, knowledge and roles. Professionals are required to take greater risks on behalf of Group B children, and this needs more trust between agencies. Such trust may be harder to establish in Group B than in Group A where the children are from families more likely to be known to other agencies and to be referred by them to the paediatrician. Group B may come from a wider range of social groups, including professionals and higher social classes. As Butler-Sloss concludes (1988 p.243) 'We have learned during the Inquiry, that sexual abuse occurs in children ... in all classes of society ...'.

There are social and resource implications of identifying Group B. Surveys of adults tell us that, as many children never disclose, there are likely to be many Group B children. Two thirds of the Cleveland children fell into this group who previously presented only rarely. Such children require specialist assessment with a relatively long involvement by the team rather than one or two investigative interviews. Increased resources are necessary if they are to be adequately assessed. We suggest that the paediatrician may be one of the few professionals who cannot avoid children in Group B because of their mode of presentation. He or she must then make the decision as to how to proceed. In our experience, the responsibility is often returned to the child, who must move from Group B to Group A via disclosure. Professionals can then avoid the conflict and risks which accompany innovative or controversial practice. This situation can be a self perpetuating one in which the issues of case management for children in Group B are never addressed and the group disappears from view. We suggest that these children will remain hidden unless and until there is a widespread acceptance of the medical diagnosis within a multidisciplinary framework. In Cleveland we found that this is self-reinforcing: corroborative information did emerge from the children. However, following Cleveland, the multidisciplinary system can respond with disbelief. suspicion or helplessness if little or no corroborative information can be found within the time limit of an investigation. It is ironic that some children were returned home by the courts with a condition of monitoring by regular medical examination. Belief in the role of the medical consultation was thus demonstrated in the service of a different agenda.

In our experience both before and after the Butler-Sloss report, there may be an attempt to discredit or minimise the medical diagnosis, effectively leaving the doctor isolated. The medical diagnosis may be incorporated as one part of the multidisciplinary team's 'diagnosis' rather than accepted as standing on its own right. The protection of shared responsibility may be chosen by many doctors whilst professional threat remains. The option of a doctor holding an opinion or concern about symptoms and signs without reaching a medical diagnosis may be helpful to those children in Group A. To have only concerns about symptoms and signs in Group B children may not give sufficient commitment to the multidisciplinary team and an ineffective investigation will ensue. The Group B child and family could easily be lost to the system at this point. Alternatives might include a watching brief, ongoing assessment, an application for a legal mandate to intervene, or a decision to try and mobilise the protective forces within the family. Options may be limited, especially for very young children or those who are very enmeshed in the abuse, who remain marooned in Group B. A wider range of creative options may follow further debate and greater experience with involvement in Group B. Such developments, however, depend on the role and validity of the medical diagnosis being accepted. This has been inhibited by media campaigns and the subsequent caution of the medical and legal professions. Since Cleveland, few viable alternatives or working models have even been suggested, let alone tested, for children in Group B and we are left only with a series of dilemmas. To resolve these, permission may be needed for mistakes to be made in case management, since greater risks inevitably have to be taken in respect of this group, particularly 'stuck' cases where the goal of disclosure may be unattainable.

Working together will create conflict unless the team members share the same level of information and theoretical knowledge, and have a common philosophy that the interests of the child are paramount. Whilst team work is needed to unravel the problems, each member of the team has a different task and thus a different focus. For example the police need to gather information from the child that is of sufficient evidential value to stand up in a criminal court and to enable them to question a suspect with conviction. This evidence needs to be beyond all reasonable doubt. A social worker or a doctor who may be required to give evidence in a civil court on behalf of a child needs to gather evidence that will satisfy a balance of probabilities. In a number of cases in Cleveland insufficient evidence for a prosecution of an abuser was taken to mean that a child had not been abused.

Child sexual abuse is above all characterised by secrecy and denial and there are societal and criminal sanctions which prevent it becoming visible in a family. These will hinder the police and social services in their search for information to support the medical diagnosis. Some assessments, particularly when the family is already known to other agencies may yield information. In other families where the abuse is well concealed and the family had not previously come to attention, the child and the doctor are likely to become isolated and trapped as described in Chapter 6 (FIG. 6.1.) In a world of adult power children may become the pawns of competing ideologies about the family. The unsupported doctor with the silent child may become pitched against societal disbelief in a desperate effort to preserve the myth of family life at all costs.

The Doctor and the Wider Social Context.

A positive response to child sexual abuse must be developed in the context of the value placed on the family as an institution. Hopefully the family can be a nurturing place for many children in the future rather than a battle field for family violence. The way forward must include help for all family members, including the abuser. The doctor's task would be to assess the health risks to the child, the social worker's to assess the safety of the client, and the police would assess the criminality of a suspected offender. Treatment resources would be available to help both victims and abusers.

At present we do not know how many, or how offenders can be safely rehabilitated with families who could then function to nurture rather than damage children. Punitive reactions against child sexual abuse may simply resemble the perpetrator's threats to the child and reinforce the hopelessness of the child's position. Nevertheless, we believe that we should aim to provide a therapeutic response within a legal framework. This may be the only way to reach some children who may otherwise silently suffer the effects of the abuse all their lives. Whilst a punitive response may be politically expedient in the short term, undetected and untreated child sexual abuse is very damaging and costly: we are paying for past child sexual abuse now at both an individual and societal level. Children are society's future and it is worth investing in services for child sexual abuse.

Conclusion – Facing Up to Child Sexual Abuse.

Paediatricians are not insensitive to resource implications, but they are also constrained and obliged to consider child sexual abuse in health terms. There is hope of support for paediatricians from adult survivors of child sexual abuse, who would have wanted their abuse prevented as children. This potential supportive lobby, whilst often silent as an effect of previous abuse, is finding the strength to speak in order to persuade society of the real extent of child sexual abuse. Without this support many doctors may accept that Group B remain hidden. If a doctor makes a medical diagnosis of child sexual abuse, a crisis will inevitably follow. Initially the parents or guardians will be shocked by the revelation of something wrong with the child. They may feel genuine concern for the child because the doctor has not assured them that all is well. However, their concern will be compounded by the implications for them of any suggestion of sexual abuse. Complex feelings will be aroused, which lead to a desire to minimise the concerns and avoid the crisis. The relatives may feel guilty that they have not protected the child, or fearful that they may be suspected as perpetrators. They may feel insecure about the effect of even the slightest concern about child sexual abuse on their whole family functioning and standing. In the course of only a few minutes all their life expectations may come crashing down. The source of the crisis is not only the possible sexual abuse of the child but the identify of the perpetrator (especially in Group B). The crisis grows with the prospect of disruption of the household by children being removed, or other members moving out. The crisis is independent of whether or not sexual abuse has in fact occurred., which may become a secondary issue. Initial disbelief and shock, the feeling of unreality, are suddenly replaced by anger. Who initiated this concern of sexual abuse? Who raised this spectre of family betrayal, suspicion, financial ruin, social outcasting and possible imprisonment? For Group B children the answer is simple: the doctor. Was the doctor right to examine the child's ano-genital region? How sure is the doctor of his or her opinion? Is it right for the doctor to speak of something so awful as sexual abuse unless he is certain? Why is this doctor trying to destroy our family? In these complicated dynamics where adults may be fighting for social or professional survival the focus can easily be shifted away from the child and onto the professional who initiated the concern.

Professionals, as well as the family, have their own crisis to face. As Glaser and Frosch (1988 p.105) point out, the timing of these respective crises may be 'staggered'. The act of raising the concern brings the two together and escalates crisis for both parties, demanding immediate action. In our belief, this is a positive move since it allows the opportunity for protecting the child. There are nevertheless risks for some children in that alerting the parents will leave the child trapped or even cause their situation to deteriorate. This has led many professionals to base their practice on containing the anxiety within the professional system until they feel that the crisis can be controlled. This course of action may be the right one for some children. Our opinion, however, based on our experience is that early action is frequently needed to help the most vulnerable children move to a position where they can be protected. We believe that this course of action for case management should remain an option as part of a flexible approach backed by a mandate from society.

5 The Continuum of Disclosure
Sue Richardson

We do have to organise ourselves so that in every case there is someone who has time and inclination to know what the child needs. (D.W. Winnicott, 1972)

Introduction

This chapter provides a framework within which to address the task of intervention. Its perspective is that the abused child's developmental level crucially influences the process of disclosure. Increased awareness of alerting signs and symptoms, together with developments in the medical diagnosis, may prompt investigation in a wide range of children, not all of whom will have made a disclosure or allegation. A sophisticated and flexible framework is needed to respond effectively to the diversity and apparent contradictions in children's reactions to what may appear from an adult standpoint to be the same situation. An additional complication is that the evaluation will often take place in an adversarial context.

Medical findings suggestive of anal penetration may be the starting point of investigation for several children. In one case there may be a vigorous denial by both the young child and possible perpetrator. A vigorous assertion that the medical findings are erroneous can lead to the explanation that the investigation produced a 'false positive'. In another, a child (again young) who spontaneously gives a recognizable account of anal penetration may be seen as confirming the precisely similar medical findings. An older child may make a hesitant statement of an activity which does not tally with the medical findings and then 'confess' to having lied. The interviewer can then be discredited in order to disqualify the child's account and draw attention away from the medical findings. The outcome of the investigation will differ in each case. A pattern of investigations characterized by just such quandries was at the heart of the Cleveland inquiry and became the subject of heated public debate.

We were privileged to work with many of the children in a clinical setting, to hear their stories and evaluate their responses. This chapter is based on the 121 children described by the paediatricians in Chapters 3 and 4, and an overlapping group of 40 children referred to the clinical psychologist over the same period of time. A high proportion of these children had not told of the abuse before the investigation. These children were either not old enough or, in our belief, not psychologically ready to tell an adult what had happened to them. Some of the dilemmas this presents for the child and concerned professionals will be considered. Both sides are seen as caught in a circular situation whereby the children cannot be protected until they have disclosed and cannot disclose until they feel safe. Our contention is that intervention will founder unless the inner world of the child in this predicament is addressed. A developmental perspective is a prerequisite to understanding the presenting pattern and creating a framework for effective intervention.

A Shift in Assumptions

Most previous strategies for intervention and treatment have been based on the assumption that the child has already moved or can be enabled to move to what Sgroi (1984 p.19) has termed 'purposeful disclosure'. This presupposes that the child is old enough to communicate and encounters the right conditions such as finding a sympathetic, believing adult.

In other words, the responsibility is mainly with the child who must take the initiative to begin the disclosure process. This renders young, pre-verbal children particularly vulnerable. The evidence is that such children increasingly present for evaluation. 27 of the 121 medical diagnoses reviewed by the inquiry were under the age of 3. The youngest sexually abused child mentioned in the report (Butler-Sloss, 1988 p.146) is a baby of 6 weeks. The youngest caught up in the crisis was aged 7 months. Gale (1988) in reviewing American studies, found that one third or more of children in case samples were under the age of 6. A study by Hobbs and Wynne (1986) of 35 children in the U.K found that 24 were aged 5 or under, with an age range starting at 14 months.

Butler-Sloss (1988, p.93) confirms that the recognition of the sexual abuse of young children is 'a new phenomenon' for professionals, highlighting the fact that, for these children, their 'plight has only just come to light' (p.5) and they are likely to present via 'non-traditional routes' (p.93). The factors cited confirm the hypothesis that as our knowledge of alerting factors has increased, signs and symptoms can be recognized at a predisclosure stage and existing models of intervention need to adapt. The inquiry found that although 'Doctors generally have not been looking at young children with the possibility of sexual abuse in mind' (Butler-Sloss,1988 p.5) , it can now form part of a differential diagnosis.

A key dilemma when using medical or other 'windows', is posed by Butler-Sloss (1988, p.7): 'if, as is often the case, the perpetrator is unknown, or is suspected but denies the abuse, how can the child be protected?'. This dilemma must be addressed in order to transfer responsibility for bringing the abuse to light from child to adult, to whom it rightly belongs. Even for adults who accept this responsibility, the task of designing effective intervention is a difficult one.

Reframing the Disclosure Process

We have found it helpful to view children as presenting on a continuum of readiness to disclose (Figure 5.1). The point which the child has reached when abuse is detected or suspected is significant because it is likely to determine the outcome of the intervention which should be planned with this in mind. Where the child has not spontaneously disclosed, it is difficult to determine the child's psychological state in advance. Other indicators or alerting signs may be present, but equally there may be none to guide the practitioner. Events in Cleveland have taught us that the key lies in a match between the child's pre-existing state, the intervention, and factors in the environment such as the presence or absence of a supportive adult in the child's family. Figure 5.1 illustrates some of the relevant factors and the concept of an interactive process of movement on a continuum.

Intervention can potentially move children in either direction. The aim should be to understand and maximize the factors most likely to move any individual child in the direction of disclosure and minimize those pulling in the direction of silence. Support for the non-abusing carer and the availability of an advocate for the child are clearly important in relation to other pressures the child may be under from the perpetrator in addition to his or her own inner psychological processes.

The Continuum of Disclosure

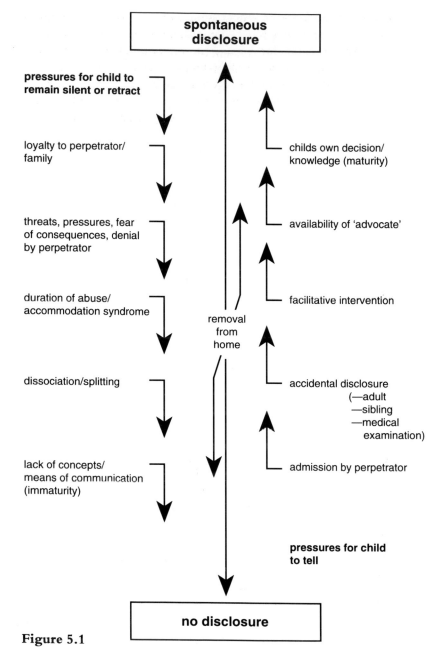

Figure 5.1

There are some forms of intervention whose impact can operate in either direction, depending on other prevailing factors. Accidental disclosure via medical examination had the effect of enabling some children to move immediately to the point of disclosure, even for children who had accommodated to the abuse. This is illustrated by Figure 5.2, based on a sample of 40 children seen by the psychologist (Bacon and Oo, 1989) which shows a strong association between medical findings and the timing of children's disclosures.

Relative Timing of Disclosures and Medical Examination

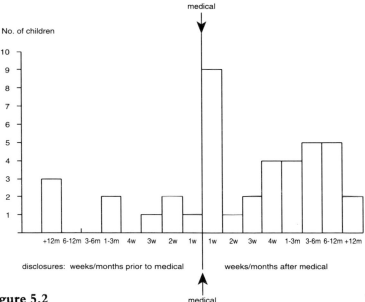

Figure 5.2

As Sgroi (1984) points out, accidental disclosure most often precipitates an acute crisis for the child, the family and the wider system. For some children, who were not psychologically ready or who were subject to strong external or internal pressures to deny, this same event appeared to have the effect of intensifying their 'stuckness' or to precipitate processes leading to denial. Removal from home had a similar effect in enabling some children to disclose but not others. An example of the latter is given by Butler-Sloss (1988, p.27) of a child who had been threatened with removal if she disclosed and who retracted on experiencing this outcome.

However, the sample of 40 children referred to above (Figure 5.2) indicates a strong association between disclosure and the provision of safety via removal from home. We see this not as a solution in itself but as part of a facilitating process. Jaudes and Morris (1990) found that the identification of the perpetrator was facilitated by hospitalization, which afforded time and space for the child and the investigators. Our experience in Cleveland of using hospital as a safe neutral environment suggested that the space provided may also help to mobilize protective adults in the family. Some mothers were thus enabled to overcome their initial shock and disbelief. Protection from the perpetrator and validation of the child as a separate person are also provided. Powell (1988) suggests that decisions on this controversial issue should be based on factors reflected in our concept of the continuum: the individual situation, the child's status and development, the maintenance of sibling relationships and the removal of the perpetrator.

Any intervention needs to enable children who are old enough to speak to move up the continuum. It is important to bear in mind that movement along the continuum is likely as part of an interactive process. All that is known about children's psychological development indicates that children actively process incoming information about external events, matching this against their existing internal perceptions of how the world works. If the child finds him or herself with too great a mismatch when contemplating a new event, she or he has the choice of changing his or her 'world view' to incorporate the new information or simply ignoring it and persisting in their original schema. Healthy children are therefore often more flexible than adults, who, as initial resistance to awareness of child sexual abuse demonstrates, often seem to ignore new information rather than change their world view. A similar process operates when a child has to deal with a trauma or stressor. A developmental model posits that children actively seek to adapt to a new situation and to develop various coping mechanisms so that the thrust of development can continue. Sexual abuse is clearly a stressor and children take an active role in creating coping mechanisms for themselves. Friedrich (1988) sees the range of children's responses as reflecting individual ways of coping in which the child will either externalize or internalize the traumatic event with various psychological and social consequences.

Driver (1988) postulates four basic ways for a child to resolve the 'moral double bind' of abuse. These are blocking, non-integration, integration or identification with the aggressor. Driver is of the opinion that the first three are determined by the messages the child receives from the outside world and the way in which he or she is responded to and communicated with during intervention. This underlines the concept of an interactive process. At the same time however, our experience is of dealing with children who had already taken up an emotional position on the continuum and whose responses varied considerably. The Official Solicitor, who interviewed children on behalf of the Cleveland inquiry, records that their reactions to the same forms of intervention 'reflected variously: "misunderstanding, mistrust, discomfort, anger, fear, praise, gratitude and sheer relief" (Butler-Sloss,1988 p.25)'. We would incline to the systemic view put forward by Bentovim (1988 p.27) that 'the pattern seen clinically depends in part on the internal 'digestion' of the experience by the individual and the way that the family and the social context processes it'.

Sexual abuse of children with disabilities and among ethnic minorities are neglected areas of study. Our experience in Cleveland did not extend to these groups. However, there is evidence, for example from surveys by Kennedy (1989 and 1990) in relation to deaf children and Brown and Craft (1989) in respect of children with learning difficulties, which suggests that children with a disability may be more vulnerable to abuse and less able to climb the continuum without the help of an adult. As Stubbs (1990) points out, a perspective on race is also needed to inform child protection work. Kelly and Scott (1986) suggest a range of clinical issues where socio-cultural factors need to be considered, affecting utilization of services, the helping relationship, perceptions and expectations. Russell's (1988) research confirms the importance of ethnicity as a factor to be considered in relation to abuse, the effects of which, she found, were more severe in Afro – American women. We suggest that in the wider context of our racist culture, upward progression on the continuum will be even more difficult for children from ethnic minority groups.

Key Groups of Children

In practice, we have found that children tend to fall into three groups on the continuum. The first group are those who spontaneously move to the top of the continuum and disclose: the second, those whose disclosure needs to be facilitated over a period of time , often under specific conditions such as safety: the third, those for whom the abusive experience is and

71

remains inaccessible, either through age or the effects of the accommodation syndrome. Summit's description (1983, pp.181-188) of the latter reminds us that disclosure is not the norm because the child's survival depends on a process of secrecy, helplessness, entrapment, delayed or conflicted disclosure and retraction. A large number of children who present for evaluation therefore probably fall into the second and third groups on the continuum. For children in the first group, already near the top of the continuum where the possibility of disclosure is greater, we contend that the tasks of intervention and treatment are theoretically easier. The children have a shorter distance to travel or may be more likely to move. They have their own momentum which helps to carry them to a point where they can engage with helping adults. For this group, there is a greater possibility of matching the intervention to the child's needs. The child has won, or is ready to win its internal battle and will permit the adult to intervene. Nevertheless, problems remain regarding the management of intervention for this group. To re-iterate Summit's findings, this group is not the norm and it is necessary to change our expectations of how victims should react. Those who do disclose may have kept the secret for a long time or made previous attempts to tell and been disbelieved. Bentovim (1988) found that over half of children who were able to disclose had been abused for 12 months or more and the period prior to disclosure could be as long as 5 years. A sample of cases in Cleveland(Bacon and Oo,1989) found that few children disclosed during the initial investigation. The crisis itself prompted many adults to disclose for the first time, figures for the Cleveland Rape Crisis Centre (1988) showing a peak of calls in the summer of 1987.

Even when the child is able to tell her or his story the disclosure is likely to be incomplete. Friedrich (1988) supports the experience of many therapists that children tend to under-report the duration, frequency and severity of abuse. Of a sample of 16 children, 6 were found to have under-reported. A further 4 began to minimize what had happened and retreat into denial, illustrating the difficulty for children of carrying the pain of the memory of abuse.

However, for children in this group, their degree of accommodation is not so great as to prevent them from breaking silence. A key factor on which the child is dependent is the response of the non-abusing carer, usually the mother, or the degree of validation received from another adult. Intervention strategies which enable the child to remain in his or her own home are then more feasible. For example, a 5 year old boy in Cleveland who disclosed to his mother that an uncle who had been babysitting had abused him, was taken to hospital and discharged straightaway because of his mother's protection and belief. Abused boys, as indicated by a review of research (Vander Mey 1988) and emerging literature such as Bolton et al (1989), may find that social attitudes, especially around gender issues, make it difficult for them to progress from the lower end of the continuum. Even where the child can readily disclose, other factors can undermine the outcome. An example is given in Butler-Sloss (1988, p.33) of how a 12 year old boy was under pressure to accommodate after disclosing abuse by his stepfather. The boy himself decided that the abuse would not be repeated and that he 'was going to make it work and behave himself'. Factors undermining successful intervention include insufficient evidence for a prosecution, even where the child can maintain his or her position, and the age of the child. By definition the decision to disclose can only come with maturity. Although young children can make clear spontaneous disclosures, problems of evidence for the courts can undermine the outcome.

The second group is where there is a high index of suspicion and the child can be helped to disclose under certain conditions. The availability of an advocate for children in this group is crucial. The experience remains psychologically accessible to the child but cannot emerge without the advocate's assistance. In Cleveland, a sympathetic medical examination by a paediatrician enabled several children in this group to move immediately to the point of disclosure, even after long-standing abuse. These children do not always need facilitative interviewing. In our experience, protection is often enough to enable them to speak. This involves, however, a degree of planned intervention which may include removal from home. The examination of siblings is also important to this group. In two families, involving a total of seven children, the abuse of siblings was discovered only following medical examination even though in each case a perpetrator had been convicted in respect of one child in the family. Children in this middle group need to be identified and offered appropriate help while they can respond. Since they may be the group able to change their position most significantly, it is vital to tailor the intervention to their individual needs. Otherwise, there is a risk of their moving down into the third group of children who remain unable to disclose, even when they present with a high index of suspicion.

Children in the third group present with very similar signs and symptoms to children in group two. They are however on a different point on the continuum in relation their inner world, external factors or developmental maturity. Very young children, without the means of verbal communication, will automatically be placed at this end of the continuum unless they have a committed advocate willing to act on their behalf. MacFarlane (1986 p.45) notes the dilemma for the child and the professionals who both may have to wait for the child to 'grow up and become more verbal before anything can be done'. To circumvent this dilemma for children who are very young, we consider that the role of the medical examination can be crucial. Our developing understanding of ritualistic forms of abuse, which induce dissociative states through fear or a deliberate use of conditioning techniques, suggests another group of children who will tend to be placed in group three on the continuum.

Another difficulty is in identifying and characterizing those children who will tend to remain stuck in response to intervention. It is clear from the accounts of adult survivors that children have previously been left to make their way along the continuum on their own. Many have found it impossible. We believe that there are dangers for this group of children in aiming for the 'middle ground' recommended by Butler-Sloss (1988,p.183). The task of setting up systems or seeking to balance interests, while helping some children, will not, of itself, provide solutions. As MacFarlane (1986 p.80) says: 'Giving abused children permission to tell secrets that they have been warned not to divulge puts them in an emotional double bind virtually unknown to children who do not carry these kind of secrets.' The defence mechanisms used to survive the abuse can be difficult to overcome. In addition, the behaviour of the perpetrator has to be considered a vital part of the equation. Research by Budin and Johnson (1989) and Conte et al (1989) found that a sample of convicted male offenders had employed a range of knowledge and strategies to select the most vulnerable victims and obtain their compliance whilst minimizing their ability to protest. The offenders indicated that some of the concepts behind prevention techniques such as 'saying no', were not likely to be effective in response to their selection and coercion of children into sexual activity. Our experience in Cleveland confirms this picture of perpetrators changing their behaviour according to the status of the child, even within the same family. Children who have been thus trapped or coerced into silence by the perpetrator or by their own internal defences against the traumatic event are not necessarily able to respond to even the most ideally planned intervention. Moreover, the needs of this group risk being overlooked or denied if we are reluctant to use assertive legal intervention.

Assertive Intervention

In Cleveland, developments in the medical diagnosis required us to face choices around intervention with children at the non-disclosure point on the continuum, where there was no guidance in existing procedures and, as became increasingly apparent , the professionals' mandate from the community was precarious. It is particularly important with children in this third group to examine the options if the dilemmas surrounding inter-vention cannot be resolved, the child fails to move and all efforts have been exhausted. It must be acknowledged that in these circumstances, it is possible to conclude that the child has not been abused; that the findings were a 'false positive'. That option can be comfortable for the involved adults, since it bestows a scientific label which allows intervention to end. It can be hard to accept this position as valid in the presence of indicators of abuse, including medical findings. An alternative is to allow the child to remain in a situation where abuse is likely, in the belief that there are no other choices available at that time. As this is a less comfortable option, efforts are sometimes made to ease it by continued monitoring. We would suggest a third option, based on a belief in the importance of acting as an advocate for the child: taking risks based on an understanding of the child's inner world in relation to other factors on the continuum. This may involve actions which are controversial such as keeping the child away from home or employing interviewing techniques which risk prejudicing the investigation. For example, as MacFarlane (1986, p.87) says:

In the best of all possible worlds, it would be advisable not to ask children leading questions, in order to avoid the concern that children are responding to suggestions that certain things occurred or that they are being compliant and acquiescent to an adult authority figure. But, in the best of all possible worlds, children are not sexually assaulted in secrecy, and then bribed, threatened and intimidated not to talk about it'. Whilst we agree with MacFarlane that leading questions which may later present legal problems are best avoided, we support her contention (p.87) that in 'the real world (they) may sometimes be necessary in order to enable frightened young children to respond to and talk about particular subjects.

During the crisis in Cleveland, we were not able to test this option to the full. Pressures such as the responses of the media, parental pressure groups and the actions of the courts, intervened to ensure that one of the first two options was preferred. The effect, in certain cases, was to create a situation of eternal argument in which no-one was allowed to break the cycle. The dilemma of unresolved intervention will be familiar to practitioners, yet there are few attempts to address it. There are no 'easy ways out' (MacFarlane 1986). A comprehensive guide to assessment for social workers produced by the Department of Health (1988) does not address this problem at all. In our opinion, a child–centred approach must allow room to provide protection for children whose version of events does not meet the criteria for belief set by adults.

As a way forward for the abused child who remains trapped in silence, we suggest paramount consideration be given to entering and understanding the child's inner world. These children are likely to be the most emotionally damaged. Some may have lived in an abusive environment for a long time and their degree of accommodation may be such that they are unable to respond to being removed from it. Other children may have repressed the memory of the abuse so that the experience has become inaccessible. These children can be severely puzzling to the intervening adult, because their lives are effectively split. Provided the child has been accurately identified as belonging to this group, a low key creative response which allows the child to unfreeze may be better than a formal interview with the time pressures of an investigation.

We need to acknowledge that the impact of intervention may cause these children to increase their defences against the pain of what has happened to them. The problems of evidence in such a case are acute. The believing adult may be under pressure to retract, with the result that such cases are lost to the system. The child is left frozen in fear, from which even the most enlightened intervention may not free them. As one survivor (Sharratt 1988) puts it, by the time help came, 'it was already too late for me – the terror had already set in'. MacFarlane (1986 p.83) reminds us that repressed memories are 'rarely retrievable during short-term intervention' and support and involvement may be required over a long period.

Child advocates finding themselves faced with these circumstances need to hypothesize about what may be happening in the child's inner world. When faced with some very accommodated children, an initial hypothesis based on alerting signs and symptoms may be all an advocate has. Adults who choose to work this way may themselves be rendered powerless to help because they may be rejected by the adult world. It may, however, be helpful to consider some hypotheses beginning with the key nature of early experience up to the age of three. At this stage of development, the child does not have the mechanisms to deal with trauma to the emergent sense of self. Miller (1987) quotes Winnicott's comparison of the infant's emotional world with that of the psychotic. Psychological survival can only be assured by repressing the memory of abuse by an adult upon whom they are dependent. The experience then becomes unconscious. Finkelhor (1986) notes the deepening of trauma over time. The effect of early signals being ignored is also described from the victim's perspective by Butler (1985). Many victims in her study felt overwhelmingly betrayed by both the abuser and the non- abusing carer for failing to recognize and stop the abuse. She describes how, by this time, irrevocable damage has been done to the developmental process and the child is unable to cope with the rage, frustration and conflict generated by the abuse.

A series of accommodations potentially follows. The child may have to idealize the abusing figure if it is someone on whom they are dependent for basic nurturance and care. That is essential for the child's survival to protect her or him from the threat of annihilation inherent in the violation by a trusted adult. Cases of extreme loyalty were noted in Cleveland. The inquiry report contains the evidence of a 19 year old who had hated the abuse by her father and had wanted it to stop but 'for my brother's sake I didn't want my family split up . . . I loved my father so much. I respected him as a father' (Butler-Sloss,1988 p.9).

For children who have had to seek ways of coping with intolerable conflicts, any attempt to dismantle their defences exposes them to the threat of unbearable emotional pain and confusion. The need to have regard to this may not coincide with the length and timing of an investigation. In Figure 5.2 it can be seen that some children needed a year or more before they were able to talk about the abuse. MacFarlane (1986 p.45) notes that the younger the child, the more time will be needed for evaluation, and months or years of work with the same person may be needed to reach the point of disclosure. How to protect children over such a long period and provide the conditions of safety which they need is a difficult issue. The decision on intervention needs to take into account what Miller stresses:

Children cannot achieve integration by themselves. They have no choice but to repress their experience, because the pain caused by their fear, isolation, betrayed expectation of receiving love, helplessness and feelings of shame and guilt is unbearable. (Miller,1985 p.313)

It may be psychologically preferable for the child caught in this situation to split off from his or her experiences and create the 'false self' described by Winnicott (1972 P.142) which acts as the 'caretaker' of the 'true self'. Miller continues:

Further, the puzzling silence on the part of the adult and the contradiction between his deeds and the moral principles and prohibitions he proclaims by light of day create in the child an intolerable confusion that must be done away with by means of repression. (Miller,1985,p.313)

Survivors who have regained their memories after many years provide a vivid illustration of this process. Constance Nightingale (1988 p.11) tells us in her poems that after 'forty-seven years of fear and hate . . . my memory returned too late'. Until then, her childhood had seemed:

like a death sentence long carried out
Memory revolts
from being involved,
like the witness of a street accident
blandly stating,
'I don't know. I wasn't there'.
(Nightingale,1988 p.3).

Sylvia Fraser's autobiographical novel (1989 p.15) describes the recovery of her memory after a similar length of time. In order to deal with the unbearable conflict caused by the sexual abuse by her father she split herself in half: 'Thus, somewhere around the age of seven, I acquired another self with memories and experiences separate from mine, whose existence was unknown to me'. Her loss of memory was 'retroactive'. She could not remember anything sexual ever having taken place and forgot each incident as it happened.

Ferenczi (1932), a contemporary and pupil of Freud, who was rejected by the psychoanalytic establishment for accepting the reality of abuse renounced by Freud, describes two psychological processes in particular which can then follow. The first is the compulsive repetition of abuse as an attempt to master the trauma. Butler-Sloss (1988,p.11) gives an example of a boy who was referred for investigation because of his sexualized conduct at school and who had to be watched all the time to prevent him from molesting other children. Johnson's research (1988 and 1989) shows that children who molest other children are highly likely to have been abused themselves. Although this may be their way of communicating what has happened to them, in our experience this possibility is not always taken seriously during investigation.

The second process identified is the introjection of guilt by the child. Ferenczi (1932, p.290) suggests that to provide protection from an unbearably negative image of the parent, the child retreats into a 'dreamlike state', a 'traumatic trance' in which the reality of the abuse does not have to be experienced. Afterwards, the child 'feels extremely confused – split, innocent and guilty at the same time', the feelings of guilt and shame intensified by the perpetrator's denial.

Summit (1983) reminds us that the accommodation syndrome is a common denominator of all victims. He also points out that there is an alternative pattern of accommodation in which the child succeeds in hiding any signs of the conflicts described above. This can easily be taken to invalidate the possibility of abuse, even where there are clear medical findings. This difficulty needs to be considered for children at this end of the continuum. An even larger number of children may be confused. Butler (1985) found that nearly all children she spoke to sensed that what the adult was doing was not right, although for some this realization might take years to dawn. This can be accompanied by a considerable degree of mystification and confusion, especially where the adult exploits the child's attachment. A survivor quoted in Butler (1985,p.31) recalls that : 'When I was small, I never thought to get angry with Daddy. He was very gentle and kind while he was touching me. He never hurt me and it usually felt nice. I was just utterly mystified about him touching me that way'. Older children at the lower end of the continuum who feel this way are very dependent on the reactions of adults and the availability of an advocate in order to understand and trust their own perceptions. Otherwise:

– if children are talked out of what they perceive, then the experience they undergo will later be seen in a diffuse,hazy light: its reality will remain uncertain and indistinct, laden with feelings of guilt and shame, and as adults these children will know nothing of what happened or will question their memory of it. This will be even more the case if the abuse occurred in early childhood (Miller, 1985, p.313).

Conclusion – Dilemmas For Practice

The framework we have outlined holds a number of dilemmas for advocates who wish to provide children with the opportunity to overcome their accommodation, speak and be protected. Perpetrator behaviour is an obstacle to a climate conducive to the needs of both the child and the intervening adult. A flexible strategy is required to meet the needs of the child who may be silenced in a tailor-made manner. The intervention needs to be equally tailored to children's place on the continuum formed by their age and stage of development, inner adaptation to the abuse and by other factors in the family and wider systems. Any part of the system is able to move in either direction on the continuum. Disclosure is therefore a process, not an event. It requires as wide a range of strategies as possible to promote and maintain movement. The dynamic is complex and involves crisis for the child, the family and the wider system. From Cleveland, we know that to resolve this crisis in favour of the child, protection is necessary prior to disclosure. We have also learned of the need for flexibility regarding different forms of protection which can be provided by the family, the legal system or a combination of the two. It is important that this range of options be kept open. In Cleveland, opinion polarized and did not allow a full choice. In the debate which has followed, there has been the danger of continued loss of freedom of movement for the child and for professional discretion to use a full range of options including authoritative intervention where this is required.

We see it as essential to face the issue of failed intervention. It is part of the dilemma of how to protect children before they have disclosed when they cannot disclose unless they feel safe. We argue for risks to be taken on behalf of children, based on a view of appropriate adult responsibility and an understanding of what is likely to be happening in the child's inner world. A framework for understanding is needed which stops the eternal search for the outside expert. Our expertise should be based on our knowledge of the experience of the children themselves and it is to this decisive source that the next chapter turns.

6 Seen But Not Heard: The Children of Cleveland
Heather Bacon

A child-centred approach to investigation must take into account before, above and beyond anything else, the context of the abusive relationship for the child concerned. (Corinne Wattam, 1989)

The concept of the continuum of disclosure can help us understand the way individual children present. In practice children can be grouped into three categories, which form the basis of this chapter. First, where the initial presentation is via a purposeful disclosure from the child, second where a suspicion is raised in another way but the child can readily be enabled to disclose during the initial intervention, and third when there is a high probability of abuse but the child remains silent despite intervention.

This chapter is devoted to children's own words and experiences, in an attempt to understand what can happen to them and to relate this to their position on the continuum at the time of intervention and investigation. Listening to children shows us that disclosure is a process rather than an event, and that children may well have a completely different framework for thinking about and experiencing what we as adults call child sexual abuse.

The child is envisaged in the centre of a series of concentric circles, the innermost being the family, the next the social context and outermost the systems for intervening in the family, i.e. the child protection agencies (see Figure 6.1).

Several boundaries have to be negotiated for children to register their plight. If this produces an unmanageable crisis, the family or other layers of the system will often be able to block the disclosure process. However, an advocate may be able to reach the child, listen to what the child is trying

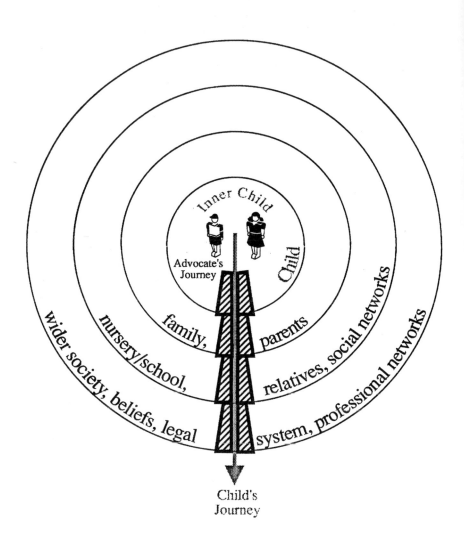

Figure 6.1

to say, and provide a safe way for the child to negotiate the boundaries. Children may get stuck at any stage, but the advocate can guide them through the layers. If the child moves to a different position on the continuum , particularly by retracting the disclosure, the surrounding networks have to decide whether to support the change. If the child moves down the continuum the advocate may accept the child's denial and move with the child, or may stay in the original position, perhaps in disagreement with the child's wishes. The advocate may himself get trapped or be disempowered. We examine this further in Chapter 8.

Group 1: Pitfalls of Permission.

Definition of the group.

Children in this group make a clear alerting statement which starts off the formal investigation, 'giving permission' for an adult to intervene. This corresponds to Sgroi's description of 'purposeful' rather than 'accidental' disclosure (Sgroi 1982 p.17). The child who reaches the top of the continuum without external help takes control of the first stage of the disclosure process by telling another person who can intervene. This is an established pathway to investigation, where medical findings (if present) may provide corroboration for the disclosure and will be seen as secondary to it :

> The child's statement is the primary source upon which to assess whether the allegation is true or not ... all other information and findings may be considered as supporting the child's statement ... in years to come there may be more concrete findings from techniques of physical examination ... but at the time of writing these do not provide certainty (Jones and MacQuiston 1988 p.43).

The process of moving up the continuum is clear in older children who decide to tell despite the pressures from years of abuse, and for younger less severely abused children who readily tell of a recent experience. Other children who give permission for an intervention may do so inadvertently, making a clear alerting statement without realising it's significance to an adult, or the events it will provoke. This would correspond to Sgroi's description of 'accidental' disclosure. The different practice dilemmas that arise may vary with the age of the child.

Examples of Disclosures in Group 1.

Girl, 15 years, who told her mother that her father was 'interfering with her'. At the police interview she said : 'He took his penis out and got me to rub it. It felt like jelly at first and then became big and hard. He had hold of my hand to rub; then sperm came out of it'.

Girl, 7 years, to her mother: 'he comes in my bed and kisses my tuppence.'

Girl, 3 years, to mother and police officer: 'Daddy wee – wees inside my fou – fou.' (What colour is the wee – wee?) 'White'.

Characteristics of Children in Group 1.

A developmental model such as that proposed by Baker and Duncan (1989) suggests an age-related progression of emotional reactions to abuse which leads to symptom formation. The earlier emotions remain but are overlaid at each stage. The progression is from anxiety (pre-school) to guilt (six years onwards) then justifiable anger (8 years on) to grief and desolation (12 years). In this model, each emotion may generate denial, which emerges as the most important internal coping mechanism for the child, or outward expression of the feelings in characteristic symptoms. Baker suggests that the stage most likely to result in disclosure is that of anger and injustice. The child may exhibit antisocial behaviours, such as violence, promiscuity, minor crime, running away, wetting and soiling, or may direct the emotion against herself, in such forms as parasuicide, secret self-destructiveness, drug dependency, or depression. We suggest that an emotional shift, similar to that seen with age, will accompany a move in the child's position on the continuum. Helping the child to move from an internalised coping mechanism, namely denial, to an externalised one where disclosure is possible, will involve gaining access to a wider range of feelings.

Older children subjected to prolonged abuse.

This model is helpful in understanding the complex inner world of children, usually approaching puberty or already adolescent, who manage to reach the top of the continuum after a long period of abuse. Of the few children in Cleveland who made a disclosure before the formal investigation, the majority were in the older age group. Older children may survive by accommodating (Summit 1983) and suppressing the experiences of earlier childhood, some parts of which may remain inaccessible to the child despite a decision to tell. This could be why some children focus on one recent episode, insisting this is all. A fifteen year old girl first told a teacher about a single event, being raped by her father one night whilst her mother was out. She did not describe a more gradual approach, beginning with suggestive teasing, progressing to touching her breasts, etc. until she felt sure that her social worker believed her and had assured her that she was not to blame. Her initial story of rape could have been dismissed as it does not fit in with the currently accepted model that most intrafamilial perpetrators carefully 'groom' the victim, creating complicity in order to ensure secrecy (Christiansen and Blake 1990).

Problems of credibility in turn lead to management dilemmas. In particular, less pressure can be brought to bear on the perpetrator if the disclosure is incomplete. Older children, with compound reactions, are often very confused about blame, responsibility, and the part played by their own sexuality. These factors can prevent a full disclosure. The child may be heavily burdened with her compliance and active participation , or her failure to disclose and prevent the abuse in the past. She may then censor the disclosure, limiting both the nature and extent of what has taken place, especially if the interviewer emphasises that what happened was wrong. A sensitive approach can help the child by 'assuming' and thereby giving permission to the child to tell of a much wider involvement, whilst avoiding statements about blame. Reassurances that the child was not to blame only apply to what is told : what was not told will remain as the part the child feels responsible for. A further reason for incomplete disclosure is that the child may have tried to tell earlier and been met with disbelief. If the child tries again it is likely to be by presenting a small piece of information, carefully observing how this is received (MacFarlane and Waterman,1986.)

Protecting the Perpetrator.

Children often seem to discredit themselves in their attempts to conceal the perpetrator's identity. One 6 year old told of being looked after on a particular night by a relative who had an alibi. The girl gave small details such as the television programme they had watched. The details of the abuse tallied with her later disclosure about her father, but the investigation foundered because her story had been transposed into a different context. Older children may draw attention to intrafamilial abuse by signalling distress about some other sexual experience. A 12 year old disclosed intercourse with her 17 year old boyfriend. Following the police interview she expressed her fear that the police 'might think it was her stepfather who had abused her.' On further questioning it turned out that the girl had regularly been shown pornographic material during access visits to her natural father. Investigation of a story of rape by an unknown perpetrator should always include questions designed to probe whether the child could be covering up for another abuser. Unfortunately it is all too easy to convey disbelief and prevent the child revealing the true picture.

Many abused children love and want to protect the perpetrator, and desperately fear losing the good parts of the relationship. They may eventually move beyond this by becoming angry on their own behalf, perhaps with the dawning realisation that their experience is not a normal part of childhood, or that the emotional closeness with the abuser was gained at too great a price. This healthy anger may at last prompt a disclosure, but the child will be devastated when the perpetrator denies the abuse and angrier still if the helpers to whom she has entrusted herself fail to intervene effectively. A child who has come this far on her journey towards potential healing may then move back down the continuum, turning her anger inwards because it is denied outward expression. This can result in self-destructive behaviour such as overdosing, arm cutting, solvent abuse and promiscuity.

This situation is vividly described by 'Alison', an 18 year old who has given permission to quote her writing. Alison was taken into care when she ran away from home at 14. Whilst in the safety of a secure unit, she disclosed that her father had abused her from the age of 6 and had also abused her sisters. However she was later returned home by social services because no appropriate placement could be found for her. Her story remained uncorroborated because her sisters who stayed in the family home denied that anything had happened to them. Alison found herself unable to prevent further abuse, and became understandably rejecting of the agencies which had failed her. She writes:

> Inside I'm like a lock and key,
> Shutting up everything inside of me
> Not being able to understand

Why I let everything get out of hand.
When the anger builds up inside of me
I'm hurting one person and that's me
'Cos I know theres two choices I could do,
Cutting my arms or sniffing glue.

In Cleveland, few perpetrators admitted the abuse even when a clear and believable disclosure was made, for instance by an articulate adolescent. Children trying to break free from the secrecy of an abusive relationship which has possessed them depend initially on the presence of a non-abusing adult in the family who will believe them and intervene. Without such an advocate the family may negate the disclosure by rejecting the child, thus putting her in the role of double victim. Only an emotionally healthy child can choose self-preservation if it means leaving the family. Some children ask the intervening agency to provide protection until they reach adulthood, but may not wish to be placed in a substitute family. L. has also given permission to quote her poems which express a series of dilemmas, the consequence of disclosing that her father's escalating demands had resulted in intercourse with her at age 15. She was placed in a family group home. She describes a happy family: 'My life before was almost perfect – our house is filled with laughter – I'm the eldest of the children and I never expected to be parted from them all..why is love used in crime, I thought my love was forever.'
L.describes her confusion over who was to blame for the abuse:

Maybe I did something he didn't like much,
Maybe my body he wanted to touch;
Maybe he thought it the wrong thing to do
But he may have felt I wanted it too.
Maybe his love for me had to shatter;
Maybe my feelings didn't matter;
Maybe he couldn't help his desires;
Maybe his emotions caught on fire;
Maybe he forgot I was a child;
He let his emotions erupt and run wild.

She contrasts her real powerlessness in the face of repeated requests with her fear of the consequences of saying no:

87

No is the word' He'does not want to hear,
No is the word that grips him like fear,
No is a word that is often said
So why is it a word which will not leave my head?
No is the only word I need to say-
But would my problems mount up or would they go away?

During the investigation L. was confused by the imbalance of questioning which made her feel she was the guilty person:

Why is the truth hard for others to see?
Why do I feel I was to blame,
Why is my heart covered in shame?
Why is it me who must do all the talking?
Why from the truth is he running and walking?
Why do I not have any more clues?
Why is this battle one I'm meant to lose.

L's father denied the abuse. The family asked her to write a letter retracting her disclosure, then she could come home again.She writes:

Would things ever be the same?
Why should I have to clear his name?
I know what happened wasn't right,
I try to push it out of sight,
I can't go and turn my story back
My words and emotions are under attack.

She described herself as 'caught in a web of hate and blackmail,loving her father but not wanting to accept his evil ways'. She saw herself as engaged in a battle – in which she was strong enough to retain her integrity.

Who'll give in first,
Who has to retract?
Who'se conscience is wearing thin?
Who needs to be matter of fact?
I'll carry on for as long as it takes,
Just accepting whatever life brings.
He is dreaming I hope he soon wakes,
There's nil on each side we go round in rings.'

A case conference decided that the medical evidence available to support L.'s disclosure would not stand up in court, on the grounds that at 15 she was old enough to have had a sexual relationship with a boyfriend and she used tampons. The investigation ended. When L. realised this she wrote:

> Proof is all they want to see
> Proof does not matter to me
> Proof it is not all intact
> Why have proof when I have fact
> Proof's what must be at the base
> They need proof for a court case.
> Proof is hidden out of sight
> I don't need proof I know I'm right.

To a child in this position admission by the perpetrator may seem even more important than her own protection. L. wrestled with a further dilemma. Knowing that the parents had refused for her younger brothers and sisters to be involved in a family assessment or to be medically examined, she told a social worker that she was worried about them. 'There are still things which happened which I have not told – when I think about whether I should tell or not I have to think whether I should put myself or my family first...I want to do what is best for them all, but whatever I do I'm still bound to fall'. L. had believed that if she allowed the abuse to continue, she would prevent her father touching the younger children, for whom she felt responsible as she had often looked after them. L's compliance with her father's demands may have intensified her feelings of guilt and despair. Her stance in insisting that she was the only one involved convinced the social workers that the others were not at risk. L. had adopted a 'strategy' of carrying the abuse outside the family, in this way leaving it intact. When she realised that other members of the family were unable to rescue her, she vividly expressed her feeling of isolation:

> Lost and alone
> In a world of my own
> There's no-one to help me now.
> I want to get out but I don't know how
> It seems that no-one feels as I do
> The situation is frightening too.
> There is no-one with whom I can talk

I get more lost the further I walk.
Things whirl round and round
I am not on stable ground
If there was someone to turn to
I'm sure that's what I'd do
A problem solved's worth more than wealth
I must solve this one by myself.

Despite the pressures for L. to retract, and her increasing isolation, she maintained her inner reality, and asked to remain in care. Eventually her mother made a fleeting contact with her. However nothing in the family changed, and L. accepted that her mother could not openly acknowledge the problem. L. chose to remain apart from her family, thereby protecting herself against further risk. In doing so she took the responsibility for all the consequences of disclosure which cost her far more than she had antici-pated. Rather than moving to a foster home, L. chose to remain in the group care home, as she felt that she could not replace her family. L. had not fully mourned their loss but still held out hope that they might change. Her story demonstrates healing despite all her pain, as the last poem in this sequence shows:

When your world falls apart it tears up your heart,
When it comes crashing down you're so sad you frown.
I've promised myself that if ever when
My world falls apart I CAN build it again.

The implications for older children facing these pitfalls are that although they may remain safe from further abuse,they are a vulnerable group who require and deserve practical and emotional support in order to achieve independent living and to resolve their anger and grief. Otherwise they may become victims of the system (Blagg 1989), drift into other abusive relationships, take refuge in denial by developing a false and impenetrable persona, seek vengeance, perhaps by becoming abusers themselves, or simply become sad. Tony Baker pointed out: 'Denials are hurdles holding people back from facing the final desolating insight -"if he could do that to me then I must have been worth less than nothing to him" '(Baker 1989).

Younger Children in Group 1.

We move now to the group of younger children who spontaneously make an alerting disclosure. We suggest that they can do so because they are less enmeshed in the abuse, which may be extra familial, of shorter duration, or less intrusive to the child, who may have a foundation of nurturance by, and trust in, adults to set against the abusive episode. The developmental model (Baker and Duncan, 1989) suggests that the predominant emotional response of the very young child to abuse will be anxiety, which in time becomes overlaid with guilt.

Children can disclose passive experiences more easily than ones they feel they shared in or initiated. We may learn more about the abusive relationship and acts from younger children who are not caught up in this dynamic. A two year old girl, in hospital for investigation of physical injury, asked a nurse to touch her genitalia. Another 8 year old girl alerted her foster parents about abuse by her natural father when she sat close to her foster father on the sofa and began to unzip his trousers. Sensing his horror, she asked 'don't you like it then?' He left her in no doubt that her behaviour was unacceptable. The next day the girl climbed into bed with her foster mother and began to caress her breasts, checking out whether this was equally unacceptable.

Children who have been sexualized by the abuse are often ashamed and distressed; it is hard for them to talk freely. One consequence of premature arousal of sexuality may be compulsive masturbation. A 10 year old girl who asked for help with this, said that she had to 'go on until she got dizzy and then sometimes she got a pain in her back like electricity'. She was distressed that this happened in school and that she felt 'she had to love whoever was there when she opened her eyes again'. Other children feel that the abuse has damaged them, so that they will not be able to marry or have babies, or that they will be disoriented sexually. One little boy of 6 years said that his father and his father's (male) cohabitee 'were poofters, and I will be a poofter too and so will my sister'. Although not strictly relevant in a single joint interview for evidential purposes, efforts to understand the child's fears can help in treatment planning.

Some children may have a condensed memory of years of abuse which have blurred into one seemingly stereotyped event. Ongoing abuse tends to follow a set pattern, with entry and exit routines, and the child may be giving an accurate account. Demands for corroborative details such as dates and place, are essentially irrelevant to the child, but may cause such confusion that her story is disbelieved. A seven year old boy who said his father had: 'stuck his two big fingers up me gap (bottom) in the dining

91

room' could give no details of time, the whereabouts of other family members, or surrounding events, and could only say : 'about twelve times' when asked about frequency.

Because young children do not possess an adult frame of reference they may make puzzling remarks, often describing what they felt, or giving an analogy. A four year old girl said that her daddy 'put a toy inside her bottom'. When her social worker asked what kind of toy, she replied 'it's an extra leg on Daddy'. Another described a knife in his bottom. The adult may need to question gently before the child can give detail which can be seen to refer to an abusive experience. For example, a 2 year old boy who initially said of a babysitter 'He bitten my Bum-bum ', when questioned by his mother elaborated : 'Tail into bum-bum'. A police interview with a 7 year old boy went as follows : 'He smacked my bum. He was poking me.' 'What with ?' 'His finger'.'Did he poke his finger inside your bum ?' 'Yes he cut me with his nail, his finger nail. He said keep it a secret or I smack you more.' Another 3 year old said 'Daddy punches me in my tummy' but after the medical examination she explained 'Daddy wees on my tummy.' It is easier to protect children who can give more detail, especially if this is supported by medical findings. Their statements give us the best 'window' into how the abuse has affected the child. The initial investigative interview is a precious and often unique opportunity, which can point to treatment needs. However information about how the child understood the abuse, any threats used, and the extent of the abuse, may be lost at this stage, because many adults,on hearing a graphic disclosure, will not probe for more information for fear of distressing the child.

Descriptions by younger, prepubertal children show the unmistakeably sexual nature of sexual abuse. Although most authors stress that child sexual abuse is primarily an abuse of adult power, we attach equal importance to the abuse of sexuality and the consequences this has for the child's sexual development (Bolton et.al. 1989.)

We must allow ourselves to hear and respond to what children actually say, as with a 7 year old girl who said 'I put my fingers up my bottom and up my front and I get feelings...I don't like a part of Daddy'. 'Which ? ' 'His tail "Why ?' 'It might hurt my tuppence'. 'Might it give you feelings?' 'Yes'. Another 8 year old had been found by her foster parents administering cream to her younger sister's genitalia, and simulating intercourse with her. On questioning she said 'It's only what me Dad used to do. He used to pull his willy with his hand, he used to put it next to my tuppence'.

'Did it hurt?' 'No' 'Were you frightened?' 'Yes I said it was hurting me and he said it shouldn't 'cos its doing you no harm.'

Some children take time to acknowledge that the abuse has hurt. Although we are aware (from perpetrators) that a gradual escalation of the intrusion can prevent major physical trauma, this is another reason why children who describe painless penetrative abuse may be disbelieved. However, the feelings may be unlocked once the child is confident that the recipient of the disclosure can cope. P. (a ten year old girl), gives this account 'He put his finger up my hole – then he tried to put his thingy up the thing where he wees out – but he couldn't. He tried to open me up a bit more, I was screaming all the time because he kept hurting me'. P. suffered recurrent nightmares and separation anxiety.

In summary, younger children who are able to tell spontaneously may nevertheless need specialist interviewing techniques to help them share their experience in an understandable way. The resulting interview may not always be acceptable to an adult-oriented legal system. The children's strong feelings may be accessible in therapy when they may be extremely angry, aggressive, overtly sexualized or sad. The child has not accommodated to years of abuse before moving up the continuum, does not have to make a decision weighing the consequences of disclosure, and, if intervention to protect the child has to mean separation from the family, there is a better chance of successful substitute parenting. There is a range of responses and outcomes for children who reach the top of the continuum, but making a purposeful disclosure is generally a healthy action for the child. However, this will only benefit the child when the self doubts and guilt are understood and an alliance is made with the child which does not break down under the pressures of the investigation. This will almost certainly mean ensuring a period of protection, sometimes by removal from home, although the family may then scapegoat the child. We have seen that older children can weigh up the damage either way and many do not wish to be returned home.

We conclude that a positive outcome is often possible for children in Group 1 but there is a risk that the child may elect, by retracting the disclosure, to move down the continuum again in response to the crisis they see themselves as producing. On the one hand, if the child is the recipient of positive and protective responses to the disclosure, he or she may start to move beyond the abuse and be receptive to treatment for its effects. On the other hand, the child may be rejected by both family and

93

external agencies in addition to carrying the unresolved consequences of years of abuse.

Group 2 : Gaining access to the experience within.

Definition of the group.

Children in this group who come to professional attention through the medical 'window' (Chapter 3), or through some other presentation, such as behavioural disturbance – in particular sexualized behaviour – rather than through an initial disclosure from the child. The child may then readily disclose provided certain conditions are met.

Examples

Boy, 9 years : Medically examined following disclosure by his sister of abuse by the father, who had been arrested and charged. No presenting symptoms or signs other than discipline problems. 15 days after the medical examination he told the psychologist 'Something going up my bum, it felt yucky and hairy, I couldn't see because I was facing down on the bed'.

Girl, 5 years : History of dysuria and complaint of buttock pain. Medical findings : hymenal opening 0.8 cm. with irregular patch on margin. Whilst in hospital she told a social worker 'Daddy hurt me with his finger'. She demonstrated with a doll.

Girl, 12 years : Medically examined after her older sister had spontaneously disclosed non-penetrative abuse by the father. Findings on examination : hymenal orifice more than 1 cm; irregular hymenal edge; reddening and oedema. After 9 days in a family group home she said 'He opened my legs with his hand and put his dick into me. He made funny breathing sounds and it hurt'.

Characteristics of the group.

A key factor in the Cleveland crisis was that children in this previously rarely seen group were referred to the child protection agencies in relatively large numbers. Action was seen to depend on obtaining a supporting statement from the child during the formal investigation. If this was to happen the child had to move up the continuum fairly rapidly. This movement may be possible for children who are old enough to overcome the communication barrier of immaturity but are not yet trapped in the secrecy of the accommodation syndrome.

The predominant emotional underpinning for this group is a compound of anxiety, guilt and anger. Consequently a wide range of reactions will occur when the child's feelings come to the surface. The energy released by this process can be part of healing, particularly when anger is positively connoted and at the same time safely contained by a trusted therapist. The reactions of the family may make it impossible for the child to go through this turbulent process without a 'safe space' created by intervention.

Some children may be helped to disclose in a facilitative interview which focuses on overcoming the child's reluctance. However, since this reluctance has its roots in the child's acute fear of crisis, loss of control and panic, a facilitative interview may make matters worse. The merits and drawbacks of this kind of interviewing are considered in more detail for group 3 children, by definition those who cannot be facilitated to tell within the time-scale of the intervention, or indeed at all. However, we often found facilitation unnecessary for children in group 2. Ensuring immediate physical protection seemed enough to help children move to the point of making a disclosure during routine interviewing; simply recognising that the child might have something to say can 'give permission' to take this step. A sympathetic medical examination can include an opportunity for the child to comment on the doctor's statement 'It looks as if something might have been happening to you down here.'(Chapter 4). A significant number of children (9 out of 32 in the group evaluated by the psychologist) disclosed immediately after the medical examination. For many others the main factor in feeling safe enough to break silence was separation from the possible perpetrator, especially but not invariably if the child had access to a supportive family member. 20 out of 23 who made explicit disclosures were living apart from the named perpetrator at the time of disclosure; only one child was able to disclose whilst living at home with an adult abuser.

We suggest that children in this group are potentially flexible and undamaged enough to accept help provided a policy of active intervention is pursued. Although this is inevitably intrusive, we have found that children can cope with the upsetting consequences and eventually reach a healthy resolution both of this and of their whole experience of abuse. This may be because, as with the younger children in the first group, the

95

abuse has been detected at a relatively early stage, and is still emotionally and psychologically accessible to the child, and because there has been a relatively short time to learn patterns of behaviour which might protect child and perpetrator in the short term but will be damaging to the child in later life. Unlike very young children who are more likely to remain in group 3, these children are old enough to communicate their experience in an understandable way. A worrying feature of this group is the demonstration that very many young children are already enmeshed in the secrecy of routine penetrative abuse and are unable to make a spontaneous disclosure.

Many children in group 2 came to attention via another child in their family rather than being a cause for concern in themselves. Various symptoms might then be recognised, such as wetting, soiling, fearfulness, insecurity, sleep disorder and regression,acting out and sometimes pre-occupation with violence and sex. One such boy, aged 9 years, was seen in a family session where his mother explained why their older sister had been removed into care. The girl had disclosed long-term abuse by her father,who had been arrested after making a limited admission. The boy, who was said to get on badly with his sister, described his intense anger at the father, saying that he would sleep sitting by the front door every night ready to 'knife' the father if he tried to return home. A younger boy sat hiding his face on hearing his brother speak. Their drawings showed large monsters eating or overwhelming small figures. After this session both children were medically examined, when signs consistent with anal penetration were found. The boys confirmed to the police that they had been abused over several months, and the older boy told of being asked to stand guard at the front door in case anyone came when his father was upstairs with his sister. The younger boy told of digital and penile penetration: 'He was sitting on my back. He got on top of me with Dad's hands on my head. He did different things – his willy was big and hairy and it stuck up P's bum, sometimes a hand sometimes a willy'. Neither child had previously told anyone.

Sometimes the child's disclosure seems bizarre and unrelated to sexual acts. Rather than risk a move down the continuum the intervention should give the child time to make the meaning clearer; this may require a structured and authoritative intervention (Chapter 2). One 8 year old girl, noted in the inquiry report as disclosing that her father and his girl friend 'squirted tea in a syringe up her front' (Butler-Sloss 1988 p.16) went on later to say that this had been a 'needle which pricked and hurted' and (several months later in therapy) that it had 'really been what Mummies and Daddies do to make a baby' but that this had been 'too rude to tell'. She said the abuse began with a game of doctors and nurses, which became Mummies and Daddies. This little girl who presented initially via her GP with a vaginal discharge, made a spontaneous statement in hospital, shortly after the paediatric examination. Medical corroboration of her report enabled the investigating team to take her story seriously. Previous attempts to tell her mother had been ignored. Once the investigation was over and she was placed in foster care, she once again became reluctant to talk, wondering whether the therapist's promise of confidentiality could be trusted. She did not want her new Mum to know the details. The time in hospital gave what might have been the only 'window' into her situation.

A four year old girl who was terrified of brushes said 'He sweeps me up with him in the bedroom, the brush hurts because he bites me with it, and he sweeps Mummy's head off with the brush' Later on :'He bites my bottom with the brush'. She pointed out a daddy doll's moustache. With safety and support children in this group can then tell enough of their experience to ensure a successful outcome in terms of child protection, but it may be many months before fuller details come to light. As with group 1, once children feel safe they may be able to acknowledge and reveal more serious prolonged abuse. One little girl of 4 years who stamped on, threw away and locked the daddy anatomical doll in a cupboard during initial interviewing, said that her mother had been 'at the chip shop' when Daddy had hurt her bottom. Later on, during a period in care whilst her mother was in hospital, she began to say that 'Mummy hurts me when she pushes the special soap into my private parts, tell Mummy not to do it any more.' The girl only began to tell of abuse by both parents after the psychologist had spent several sessions crouched in a large cardboard carton, obeying the child's injunction not to look whilst she re-enacted and gained control of the experiences.

It is important to remember that children in the same family can be at different points on the continuum. Thus an older child who reaches the top of the continuum can be scapegoated as 'seducing' her father, and, whilst attention is focused on helping the mother move to a less punitive position, younger children can remain locked in secrecy about ongoing abuse.

We experienced this pattern in Cleveland. In one family where the father had been previously convicted and older children disclosed non-penetrative abuse, the younger children showed no sign of disturbance and were deemed 'too young to know' what had happened to their sisters. However, medical examination revealed signs of penetrative abuse which the children disclosed on being taken into care. The power of this family to close ranks and maintain secrecy was such that the mother, although participating in family work where she heard her pre-pubertal daughter describe being raped and her 6 year old son describe being digitally penetrated and threatened with murder, later went on to assert that there had been no abuse. These two children then retracted their disclosures and eventually the family was reunited. Helping the children to move up the continuum had only a limited value in the longer term when the social services had no mandate to intervene further. Professional disputes about this demonstrated 'conflict by proxy' (Furniss, 1983) which added to the difficulty of matching intervention to the children's positions on the continuum.

In summary, for group two children, years of further abuse may be prevented and the child could be helped, provided the intervention is authoritative in ensuring protection from ongoing abuse and from the reactions of others to the crisis of disclosure, and supportive of the child's need to express difficult emotions. Without intervention, the child would have to make his or her own way up the continuum with the concomitant risks of being overcome by the processes of accommodation and denial.

Group 3: Trapped in Silence

Definition of group:

Children in this group present without prior disclosure, but with indicators of abuse, particularly medical findings, which must be taken seriously. On investigation the child is unable to disclose any evidentially acceptable details of abusive experiences, or may completely deny them.

Examples.

Pre-pubertal girl, 9 years: recurrent urine infections from 3 years, daytime wetting, history of intermittent bleeding which mother thought was menstrual. On examination, intact hymenal ring admitting index finger (1.5cm), rectum fissured and dilated. The girl vehemently denied that anything could have happened although her mother had told the social worker of her own worries.

Girl, 11 years: hymenal opening ragged at 7 o'clock position, introitus 2cm. This girl, who had presented with hysterical fits and night terrors, was extremely distressed on gentle questioning (during a clinical session rather than an investigation), and repeated 'nothing has happened, I would tell you if it had'.

The second opinion of a police surgeon was that the findings on both girls were within normal limits. Policy at that time (late 1987) dictated that intervention could not proceed on medical grounds without prior agreement on the significance of the medical findings. No case conference could be held, and as neither child disclosed they both remained at home with no further action.

Characteristics of the group.

The children come to professional attention indirectly, perhaps via a disclosure from another child, often a sibling, who has witnessed or been involved in abuse, or because of medical findings which suggest chronic penetrative abuse (see Chapter 3),or venereal disease, or rarely, an admission by a perpetrator. Despite protective intervention they remain unable to speak.

Doyle (1990,p.1) gives convincing reasons for the paradox of children in the group, who apparently resist rescue : 'Many seriously abused children will defend their parents, guard the family secret, and try to avoid removal from home'. Like victims of kidnap and captivity they depend on their abusers and may come to feel responsible for them. Continuing abuse can lead to despair and to helpless behaviour even when chances of escape are offered.

The children may have fragmented memories due to the repression of their experiences (MacFarlane and Krebs, 1986 p. 83).The presence of such memories is indicated by avoidant reactions and negative associations to material presented by the investigator. Repression acts later as the 'psychological time-bomb' frequently reported in the literature. It also functions as an important survival mechanism for children who do not see disclosure as an option at the time of the abuse (Macfarlane 1986.)

Some children in the group will be pre-verbal : one little girl was seen because her six year old brother gave the following description of the father's behaviour on access visits: 'He sticks his tail up D's fou-fou, his tail is bumpy'. On examination the three year old girl had physical signs of a scarred lower vaginal wall but an intact hymen. She had not disclosed but suffered from sleep disturbance, stomach ache and bedwetting, and her mother had noticed rectal bleeding.

Older accommodated children in the group rarely present for evaluation until the medical 'window ' provides a way in. They evince the greatest puzzlement, confusion and controversy, because the key to reaching and helping these most damaged children lies in understanding why they deny abuse. Attempts to help the child break silence may be met with misunderstanding and sometimes hostility. The problems have been well documented in the literature: 'It is extremely important to realise that children rarely lie about sexual experiences, except to minimise their involvement' (Stone et. al. 1984). Children involved in ritual or satanic abuse are likely to fall into group three, because sophisticated and psychologically destructive techniques are used to silence them, including forcing the children to abuse one another and commit destructive acts (Dawson and Johnston 1989).

Children in this group present us with the most difficult dilemmas in child protection. If, for example, strong suspicion is raised by a medical examination, but the child denies or cannot speak of abuse, one has to conclude that either the medical findings have been wrongly interpreted and no abuse has occurred (a false positive), or that the child has been abused but something is preventing him or her from saying so. Experience in Cleveland seems to indicate that the process of investigation and entry into the legal system makes it more likely that the first view will prevail.

However, in the case of some children who did not immediately return to their families, those who cared for and talked with them slowly became convinced that more probably they had been abused and effectively silenced. This applies particularly to a group of girls, in the middle years of childhood, with signs of chronic genital and anal penetration. (In the group evaluated by the psychologist none of these children disclosed. They may correspond to children described by Wynne and Hobbs (Butler-Sloss 1988, p.318), who are at the crossover point where with increasing age, anal abuse becomes less common and genital abuse more likely.

The mother's position is crucial for group 3 children, who may feel that she is the only person who can 'give permission' for them to disclose. The mother may find herself in an impossible dilemma : Butler-Sloss (1988, p.8) comments that 'in the conflict between her man and her child, the relationship with the man, the economic and other support which she receives from him may disincline her to accept the truth of the allegation'. The problem is worse when, as in this group, the child cannot say anything directly or clearly to the mother about sexual abuse. It will seem to be a choice between the word of the professional and the possible perpetrator. Mothers in Cleveland became subject to public pressure, the media portraying them as 'innocent parents' rather than separate individuals : any dissociation would imply that their partner was guilty.

How can a non-abusing parent in this situation support a child against her partner? When the public crisis reached a height, news cover was intensive and virtually one-sided. This was later mentioned in the Butler-Sloss report (1988, p.171) : 'the impact of the reporting . . . .can have a disproportionate influence on those caught up..and may create uncertainty, confusion and injustice'. Social workers felt that the media coverage 'created even more difficulty for some parents attempting to accept and believe what their children were saying,..leaving the children confused, vulnerable and in some cases totally unprotected ' (Nelson and Long, 1988).

Many of the children may have watched on television their parents' public denial of abuse. They realised that a drama was being enacted. This enhanced the pressures for family loyalty and denial. Despite this, some mothers still managed to support their children. One six year old girl, for example, who had gross physical signs of anal and vaginal abuse, initially named her grandfather but then became reluctant to say anything. She was admitted to hospital for investigation, her mother choosing to stay with her. Confusion arose when the signs reappeared even though the grandfather was living in a bail hostel following the initial allegation (Butler-Sloss, 1988 p.14). The mother agreed to suspend visiting by all male members of the family while a further investigation took place. In hospital S. was frozen, fearful, and regressed. She insisted on staying wrapped in a blanket. The mother came to realise that logically the perpetrator must be her husband and felt able to hint to her daughter, so as to give her permission to tell, that 'she had an idea who it might be'. That night S. gave her mother an unmistakeably sexual tongue kiss and when asked who had taught her, she spelled out the letters 'Daddy'. S. subsequently wrote this down during an interview with the psychologist. She was never able to write or say more than that : 'Daddy had hurt her bottom with his fingers on the inside', but her drawing of 'Daddy when he hurt her' gave many clues as to what had taken place. She pointed to the penis in her picture saying 'and then he gets his razor out'.(Figure 6.2)

She declared that as she had been asleep she hadn't been able to see what happened. This was a common assertion, and may be a distancing mechanism, perhaps protecting the child from the feeling of active participation. In any case sleep probably precedes and follows the event for many children abused at night. No further police investigation took place but S. remained safe from further abuse, initially whilst she stayed in fostercare and later at home under wardship conditions. Interestingly the wardship judge decided not to hear the case, saying he felt he would be unable to reach a satisfactory verdict on the available evidence. This little girl had the benefit of a supportive parent,but remained unable to talk freely about her experiences. She said later, on watching a television programme about the crisis, 'I was a child sex abuse wasn't I Mummy but I'm not now'.

The tasks involved for a mother to become an advocate for her child are addressed in more detail in Chapter 8. Conerly (1986) emphasises the process of 'teaming' with the mother, who will be in crisis after the disclosure. This may provide the best protection for the child in the future but may create immediate problems for the mother in separating from the perpetrator, nurturing the children over this period, and making practical decisions. Unless greater emphasis is placed on giving support without separating mother and child, mothers may have to turn to other sources of support, such as the perpetrator. The advantages of leaving responsibility with the mother throughout the period of disclosure must be weighed against the danger that she may be unable to resist the pressures for denial from the perpetrator or other family members.

If the mother's position is ambivalent or unsupportive the child depends on the external system for help. In Cleveland, such children fared less well. Although the process of accommodation to long-term abuse has been well-described in the literature (Summit,1983, Sgroi,1982, Bentovim, 1988), the concept may be lost during legal proceedings. Lack of regard for children as people may underpin the prevailing climate of public opinion. This was shown by press coverage of the Cleveland crisis which seemed

Figure 6.2

to assume that the main issue was a dispute between parents and profession-als (Newell, 1988). In the words of Butler-Sloss (1988,p.95), 'The voices of the children were not heard.' Children who remain unable to speak for themselves and lack the support of a believing parent require advocates who can cope with their confusion and contradictions. As yet, the views of the child's advocate may not be given equal weight with those acting for the parents. This can create profound difficulties: 'If public agencies abandon the family when it becomes clear that a legally provable case cannot be made,their actions become part of the problem '.(Taubman, 1984).) Children are then caught up in a process of denial by the wider system, which in turn compounds their problems. Outside experts may be asked to comment, and may sometimes give opinions, based on indirect evidence, which are not truly child-centred and which do not take into account what is known about the processes of accommodation and retraction (Vizard et.al.1987).

Group 3 is characterised by polarisations and contradictions in medical diagnosis, psychiatric opinion, and interpretations of what children ac-tually say. For example, a pre-pubertal girl who had been examined following a medical diagnosis of sexual abuse to her brother had medical findings of 'gaping vagina, fixed open, hymen absent 1.5x1cm., anus lax, reflex dilatation to 0.5cm, with scarring 6 and 12 o'clock'. The second medical opinion was that this was 'consistent with digital or partial penile penetration; a third by a police surgeon was that the 'findings were within normal limits'. The child said virtually nothing on initial examination, but had confirmed on gentle questioning by the doctor that 'something had been poked up her bum and up her fanny,' said that this was 'several times . . . over a long time' and that 'a grown-up living in her house' had been responsible. She later confirmed her brother's statement : 'I don't know what's happened – if it's happened – Dad might have put his penis up our backsides . . . this is how it really was' (demonstrating with anatomical dolls). A judge who saw videotapes of the interviews concluded that 'the children had not and did not disclose'. An independent psychiatrist acting for the parents said,'So far as the children are concerned I think it inconceivable that they could have withheld details or hints of what had happened if they have actually been abused'. The children said that what happened must have been at night. The psychiatrist added 'In my opinion anal penetration and even less intrusive sexual abuse is very unlikely to occur during sleep'.

The pressures of the investigation are impossible for children like this, who remain at the bottom of the continuum. The best chance for them to talk is probably right at the beginning, as they soon become even more trapped by the family reactions. Sensitive and specialised interview techniques may be the only way to reach them, or alternatively, a chance to talk in the clinical setting before a formal investigation is started. There is inevitably a worry that the child will be silenced even at this stage. Problems in the initial investigation can consign a child to group three from the start. A pre-pubertal boy who was medically examined following a diagnosis of abuse to a brother, showed signs on examination thought to be consistent with sexual abuse: 'anus lax, reflex dilatation to 0.5cm., scarring to give smooth shiny skin, peri-anal redness, deep fissures 12,2,5,7, and 9 o'clock.' Until that time, no concerns had been raised about the child and the only history of note was a previous referral for behaviour problems. The second opinion was that the medical signs were consistent with 'chronic anal abuse with penetration'. Like the majority of children caught up in the crisis, during the formal investigation that followed he was unable to tell of anything that had happened. The key to why may lie in what he later said to the psychologist about the police interview: 'The police seemed to blame it on me. At first I didn't really believe it when they said it was me, and now I feel slightly angry that it was like that . . . You see, Dad sat with me when the police interviewed us'. It never became clear whether this boy had, as he put it, 'done something slightly by mistake' to another child in the family. However, the police concentrated on this aspect, accepted this as the likely explanation of medical findings for the other child, and in the absence of any admission by an adult, closed their investigation. They sought no explanation for the medical findings on the boy.

A dilemma arises in such cases, when no perpetrator is identified. In Cleveland, social services felt bound to act on what they saw as valid evidence of sexual abuse. In order to protect children, and to carry out further assessment of both children and parents, child protection procedures, including place of safety orders, were invoked. Where the perpetrator could not be identified or a protective adult found in their family, the children might be placed in foster homes. Some children in this situation were then seen regularly, by clinical psychologist/social work team, over a period of weeks after the formal investigation had been ended but prior to any decisions by a court as to whether they had in fact been abused. The children have been described as 'double victims – of abuse and of well meaning but misdirected and harmful responses to it.' (Newell,1988). However, despite the trauma of separation from their families, many children, although remaining unable to speak directly, expressed relief that they were protected. One girl, who agreed that 'she had had some bad touches in her private parts', concurred with her mother 'that one good thing was that it had stopped' and told us that her recurrent nightmare of 'wolves with long noses coming into her room' had gone and that she felt 'sad and glad' to be in care. However, children who have been threatened with leaving home if they tell of the abuse, may react quite differently and vigorously deny that abuse has occurred.

Group 3 children often spoke in an oblique way. One highly intelligent and articulate boy at first seemed unaware of any past event that he could understand as abuse, but said that he 'believed what the doctors had told him,' that: 'He had marks in his private place and someone had put something in to cause the marks'. He 'did not know what had happened', however; 'it must have begun before the family had moved house'; several years previously. He spoke hypothetically, prefacing his remarks with 'if it has happened'. The team adopted the same style, encouraging him to explore what might have happened. This approach has been described by the team at Great Ormond Street (Vizard et. al. 1987). It does not depend on the child making a spontaneous, unled statement, but aims to talk about abuse in a way that enables the child to speak. This has been much criticised, as inappropriate, misleading or leading, and there are doubts as to whether evidence obtained in this way can be legally helpful or valid (Waite, 1987). Nevertheless it may prove to be the best way of helping some children, as in this instance when the child began to say 'what might have happened', volunteering that it was 'probably at night, when 'Mum could be out' and 'if it was M. (brother) it could be any time because Mum might take me shopping and then Daddy would look after M'. Whilst prefacing his remarks with 'if it happened', he demonstrated a remarkably sophisticated reaction which convinced us that this was a protective mechanism : he was unable to betray his abuser directly.

Conversations with children in this group help us to understand the cognitive and emotional tasks imposed on them when the abuse comes to light. The abuser may have taught the child that the experiences he has undergone are normal and unimportant, whereas the interviewer will regard them as significant and unusual. The child will therefore have to adjust his whole viewpoint. Vizard and Trantor (1988,p.116) give help and guidance for therapists working with such conflicted anxious children. They point out that 'no matter how long the therapist allows for the child to name the alleged perpetrator, this simply will not happen',and that facilitation of some kind is necessary. Even when it has been established that abuse has taken place there is a risk that the perpetrator is wrongly identified. In our experience this is a real risk, as children do try to protect the perpetrator. Sometimes the interviewer can help children by reassuring them that this difficulty is understood. This is a perilous path for the interviewer, who will be perceived as prejudging the issue, but it is a child-centred way to help the frozen and anxious child over the block created by the denial process.

MacFarlane and Krebs (1986) also advocate the use of hypothetical questioning: what does the child think an experience would have been like if it had happened ? This can help children who deny abuse especially where answers are needed urgently and the child cannot be left to come to a direct disclosure in his own timescale. The difficulty of breaking the secret is forcibly brought home to us by children who talk about their fears for the family. One child who named his father 'Although I'm not saying that he has done it', broke down in tears, after a while managing to say 'I'm frightened – I'm frightened about Mummy – I feel so sorry for her'. He went on to talk of his fears for the emotional and economic position of the family if his revelation led to divorce. At this stage it is vital to understand and give reassurance that these are adult responsibilities.

Some children want the task of disclosure to be taken by a protective and more powerful adult, in the hope that the perpetrator will then be enabled to confirm the child's allegation: 'I think, if you tell him, I think he did it to us, Dad might say who it is as well.' This is the point at which an advocate for the child must be willing and able to take over, thus helping the child with his burden. The problem in doing so is that the disclosure may be partial and hypothetical, with few or no details of what actually happened. Nevertheless the child has reached a vital point and his effort must be 'marked' in some way. Telling the child that a partial disclosure is believed has ethical implications. Butler Sloss (1988,p.205) comments 'In Cleveland there was confusion as to whether some interviews were conducted to ascertain the facts or for therapeutic purposes or a mixture of both. It must also be clear whether it is intended to facilitate the child to speak and if so in what way'. However, a child-centred professional approaches any interview with a therapeutic aim, whether or not facts are ascertained, or a legal decision has been made as to whether there has been abuse. In some cases where abuse had not been proven, this sort of interview was heavily criticised for placing an intolerable burden of emotional abuse on the child. Such comments may reflect the distress experienced by adults on witnessing the child's pain. The real significance is that despite the pain and the absence of detail, the child has shared the experience. This means he can transfer to others the responsibility he carried, for keeping the secret for himself and for his family. In acknowledging that his experience is perceived by us as sexual abuse, the child entrusts us with the task of acting on his behalf. The ethical considerations here are almost overwhelming. How is any child to handle such an accidental disclosure which intrudes into the child's life and may require him to dismantle his defence, coping mechanisms, and eventually his perceptions and cognitive framework?.

It is difficult to convey the certainty experienced in this situation that the child's emotion expresses a profound relief. This may be disqualified as simply a projection on the professional's part of the relief at finding an explanation. However we feel sure that at such moments we are the recipients of a momentous communication, with the power to alter things positively for the child. This feeling characterises all the purposeful disclosures we have received from children in the middle years of childhood,and also from previously silent adults. It cannot easily be shared with a court or conveyed adequately in legally acceptable terminology. The admission of videotaped evidence as recommended by the Pigot Committee (1989) would greatly assist in child advocacy and in the central task of conveying the child's position to the court.

Another way to help the child who feels powerless is by confronting the denial which invariable operates in the family when children have been abused in secrecy over a long period. MacFarlane and Krebs (1986,p.171) describe a way of doing this:

> Some non-abusing caretakers and parents,(particularly those in incestuous situations), are so disinclined to believe an interviewer's impressions or conclusions, and so unwilling to accept even the possibility of abuse, that it may be useful to show them the videotape . . . (of the interview) out of the presence of the child.

We were criticised by parents in Cleveland for employing this strategy which they saw as deliberate cruelty. One mother said that a video clip of her child 'had said nothing to her'. How should we mitigate the pain of such a confrontation, without lessening the urgency we feel about obtaining help for the child from an adult who loves him? We must also acknowledge our own confusion and reactions when a parent is unable to take the step of believing. The professional must remain aware of the possibility of her own anger in response to the fact that a mother in such a situation may not behave in a way that might be expected or desired.

Some children who can acknowledge the medical findings of abuse may then begin unlocking the experience. The following conversations took place after medical findings of abuse in a brother and sister both under 11 years:

Interviewer: 'Would it just be a normal thing that happened in your family do you think?'

Child: 'Yes . . . .I think we would have thought that it was just happening to us on the spur of the moment – probably it was only happening to me.'

Interviewer: 'You wouldn't have been able to say to anyone else?'

Child: 'The first few times it happened, then I would have thought about it, and then I would have just forget about it, it would be routine, and then I might not be able to tell you straight away that it is..He might have said, forget this has happened today, it will be our secret.'

Interviewer: 'I wonder what Daddy would have thought, what would happen if it wasn't a secret?'

Child: 'That he'd get into trouble.'

The boy said he thought the same might have happened to their father as a child: 'Daddy might have thought it was a normal part of growing up, that could be why he might have done it'.

Girl: 'But now he, since he's been married he would know it was wrong.'

Boy: 'He would know; he couldn't change'.

Such sophisticated conversations show how well children understand the dynamics of secrecy, and the consequences of disclosure. It is important to establish whether the child still feels at risk. One child in foster care had described his uncertainty about past abuse: 'I don't think I knew what was happening to me . . . I might have sort of imagined, instead of seeing what was really happening, maybe sort of being awake but like a strong dream or something, sort of being in a trance . . . A trance is when something's happened and you – it's like being hypnotised, you believe not that it's happened.'

Interviewer: 'How do you think you might have got into the trance?'

Child: 'He might have said, go back to sleep or something like that . . . Go back to sleep, I'm just coming to fetch something from your bedroom.'

Interviewer: 'Do you think that if you went back home again – ?'

Child: 'I think I would start to know really because just say if we went back, now we know it's happened we might not fall asleep so easily, and be anxious . . . '

One ten year old girl was quite certain of why abuse would continue:

Interviewer: 'Do you think if you went back home it would happen again?'

Child: 'Yes. But the abuser might wait a while, so we sort of half forget it.'

Interviewer: 'What makes you think it wouldn't stop altogether?'

Child: 'Well, say I was pinching biscuits, I can't stop pinching biscuits. Might be an addiction. If the abuser's done that, he can't stop.'

Interviewer: 'Do you think anything could help him stop?'

Child: 'Yes. If the abuser said it was him. Or if he got some help – if he gained help. And then, he might feel sorry for the children, and all the worry we've had, and he might, part of him could recognise, it's a bad thing, and he shouldn't really do it . . . Well I wondered about us all talking and things'.

It seems that relatively young children can have a clear idea that although the sexual behaviour is the adult's responsibility and is damaging to the child, the adult is himself unable to control it.

Children in this group do not see disclosure as a real possibility. Two pre-pubertal children who were examined and taken into care following diagnosis of sexual abuse of another sibling, were asked 'What do you think

would have happened if X (younger child) hadn't gone to see the doctor?
Girl: 'It would just of carried on.'

Boy: 'I think after a couple of years, when we were older, we might have
found out what had happened and we might have had the courage to tell
somebody'.

Interviewer: 'How old do you think you might have been before you were
able to work that out?'

Girl: 'I think just about married'.

Boy: 'I think maybe we'd have to be in the senior school'.

Girl: 'Just about leaving'.

Boy: 'No not just about leaving, about maybe two or three years on from
now. Because if you'd been older, then you wouldn't spend so much time
in the family and then you wouldn't be so prone to this happening and you
wouldn't be so docile to it'.

Girl: 'What does docile mean?'.

Boy: 'Fragile, that's really the word, it's because, like if you're a slow
runner and there's a fast runner, you can be easily caught can't you in a
game of tig, but the older you get your're more mature . . . you've got
more freedom then'.

Children trapped in silence may be convinced that nothing significant has
happened to them, because their perceptions have become distorted
through the accommodation syndrome. The following conversation
suggests this:

Interviewer: 'Say if you decided that you wanted to tell someone. How
would you start to tell do you think?'

Girl: 'I'd probably say, um, can I talk to you in private, and then I'd say –
I'd try to get to know you first – and then I'd say, someone's been abusing
me, in a certain way, and then, I don't know what to do about it, what do
you think I should do, and then, can you help me please'.

Interviewer: 'And what would you say to convince us, we need to know
a bit more than that.'

Child: 'I might have gone to a doctor to convince me, to make sure whether I was right or whether I was making it up, to make more certain; like Dr.X's photos and that.'

Interviewer: 'We might not be sure what you were talking about.'

Child: 'I might say how I'd been abused. I don't know really.'

Interviewer: 'What do you think we'd need to know before we could do anything to help?'

Child: 'Um – who it was.I'd say, and then ,probably, write it down on paper maybe, or say it very quickly..if I said who it was, . . . '

Interviewer: 'Go on then . . .'

Child: 'Daddy.'

Interviewer: 'How do you know it's Daddy I wonder?'

Child: 'I just know.'

It is easy to see how adults (in this case, the mother) could disbelieve the child on the grounds that 'the doctors have put words in her mouth'. In fact the child may be seeking to validate the unbelievable by reference to an authority figure who can have equal weight with the parents. In this case the child later shifted stance in line with that of the father, who told her that he did not believe the abuse. The child replied,' I only accept that I've been abused because I've been told by the doctors'. A confused and frightened child cannot resist such re-framing, which will lead to retraction of the disclosure in many cases. Such children seem to inhabit a topsy-turvy world where they are uncertain of the validity of their own experiences. A vehicle of expression which does not depend on words may be helpful. Older children in this group were aided by the use of anatomically correct dolls, a technique usually reserved for much younger children.

A similar confusion for the child about whether forbidden things really happen or not was shown by a six year old girl who presented with sexualized behaviour. When telling of an assault by an older child in the neighbourhood she reported that her much older brother had said 'It's alright for your big brother to do this but not for someone outside the family'. When questioned as to whether her big brother had done anything, the child said 'I don't think he has done really because Mummy would be cross if he did.'

The child's need for secrecy to protect the abuser can involve a delicate balance when there are other vulnerable siblings or adults. Sometimes children may be helped by an analogy of the family on a see-saw, with them at one end and the abuser at the other. The children are asked to place themselves to show whom they are protecting. In one family a girl who had made a partial disclosure placed herself at the opposite end, i.e. not protecting the abuser. Her brother placed himself in the middle, i.e. balanced between protecting the abuser – by not telling – and the younger children – by telling. After making a partial disclosure himself he moved his position to the end with his sister and crossed out the word 'abuser', replacing it with 'Dad'. The mother was then able to respond to this by saying that she had been at the middle point but could go on to place herself at the end with the children.

Some children become so dissociated from what has happened that they cannot recall the abuse. Two children, a girl aged 10 and her brother aged 8, whilst initially able to tell of penetrative abuse by their father, later 'forgot' about it during the investigation. The girl later changed her christian name, and the boy could only describe events in the third person, talking of abuse to an imaginary boy he named 'Peter'. An older brother had however witnessed the actual abuse. The younger boy and his sister were already distancing themselves from the abuse by choosing different names. This is reminiscent of those adults who develop multiple personalities in response to the need to keep part of the inner person intact, or to split off the angry feelings. Although it is difficult to understand how such experiences can be forgotten, many adult survivors report loss of childhood memories. In group 3 children the experience may already be inaccessible. MacFarlane and Krebs (1986,p.84) comment further :

> Children who we have reason to believe have repressed abuse, i.e. where there are clear medical findings of abuse, where the child re-enacts molestation in play, or where there is evidence to suggest that all other children in their circumstances, especially in their family, were abused, usually need time and the emotional support that only long-term treatment can give.

This can be misinterpreted by expert witnesses, who may conclude that a mistake has been made: a false positive.

Commentators have concluded, in respect of such children in Cleveland, 'Some children who were clearly not sexually abused were retained in the system far too long' (Bagley and King,1990). This statement highlights a central confusion which recurs whenever the events in Cleveland are debated. Since Butler-Sloss (1988,p.183) found herself unable to consider the question of whether individual children had been abused, the public has been left in doubt. This has made it impossible for anyone to decide whether the cases were appropriately managed or not. In response to this situation we have chosen in this book to address the case management of abused children who fall into group 3. We accept that, as we ourselves did, all professionals must bear in mind the risk of false positives. At the same time we are concerned that this prospect may cause unnecessary alarm. This anxiety needs to be balanced by our knowledge that the reaction of non-abused children to investigation is significantly different, provided the investigation is skilled and sensitive.

Unlike group 2, where the provision of a place of safety or separation from the likely perpetrator often allowed children to disclose, group 3 children seemed to have insurmountable, internalised injunctions for secrecy. They were too young to contemplate leaving their family, or to survive the wrath of the perpetrator, or rejection by their mother. They therefore became terrified of the consequences of disclosure, and although they may have begun speaking initially, would quickly realise that their family could not cope, and move to a protective position for them. Physical separation from their family was unbearable, and led them to say what they perceived would allow them home again, i.e. that nothing had happened. The dilemmas for professionals in this situation centre around how much work should ever be done without a legal mandate. It may have helped some group 3 children in Cleveland that in the short term their experience was validated, and what they said accepted, although in the end this was disqualified by the wider system and by their families. Whether the process left them better protected, or simply more trapped, remains an unanswered question.

Practice Issues: Matching the Interview to the Child's Needs

One important and overlooked factor in children's response to an interview or investigation may be the way the children perceive the power discrepancy between themselves and the worker. Children need to feel strong and safe enough to tell, or to take a calculated risk that telling will result in safety. However, the child trapped in abuse is likely to be deeply mistrustful of adult power. In Cleveland we took the overall view that the adults directly involved with the child had to be seen as equally powerful with the perpetrator before the child would be able to entrust them with any secrets. This view was also held at that time by experts in the field (Sgroi, 1985, Bentovim, 1988). An approach which involves exerting a degree of pressure on the child to overcome the resistance created, for example, by the perpetrator's threats, can easily be maligned or misunderstood. We think that an authoritative approach, where the adult interviews the child in a leading way, may work well for children who are towards the top of the continuum (Chapter 5); they will recognise that such an adult has the power to confront and be angry with the abuser. The child may furnish clues as to whether he sees the situation in this way when asked about whom he wants to tell, and how he sees the consequences. In Cleveland we heard several children question plain clothes police officers doubtingly about whether they really were policewomen, with uniforms and police cars to catch baddies. Before one 5 year old decided to tell, he played out a repetitive game over several weeks of summoning police, fire brigade and ambulance to rescue him and arrest his father.

On the other hand, many children at the developmental stage of anxious dependence on the abusing adult will only be helped by an adult whom they can perceive as being at their own level. In this instance a police uniform will not be helpful, nor will a discussion of what might follow from the disclosure, although as Butler-Sloss (1988 p.245) points out, children are entitled to a proper explanation appropriate to their age and should be given some idea of what is going to happen to them. To achieve a relationship on equal terms with the child the advocate must be in touch with their own inner child. This does not mean being out of control in any way, it simply involves giving the child a safe space where no adult agendas intrude. Central here is the ability to ask questions in a way which clarifies what the child presents, without directing or interpreting it. Children can sometimes feel better if they block out all external reminders that they are telling a secret. Distancing themselves from the telling can help. One child whispered the secret to a puppet representing a favourite children's TV character. As the puppet could only squeak rather than talk the child was then persuaded to tell the interviewer what the puppet had 'heard'. The task of telling a secret can sometimes be

115

re-framed. One child we saw had so many fears of noises outside, constantly startling and distracting herself with them, that in the end the interviewer said: 'that's just a tractor, he is just doing his job, and that is just a lawnmower, and that is just an aeroplane, etc.etc. and they are all doing their jobs, and your job is to tell me about what happened'. Whereupon the child said, 'Thats my *job?*' She then proceeded to tell. These techniques, sometimes quite directive, can be embedded in a more open-ended play session. This may help children when a more facilitative interview is likely to be perceived as threatening.

There are even greater difficulties in matching the type of interview to the needs of children at the bottom of the continuum: an undirected, child-led session may leave them trapped in silence. Facilitation, which, without exerting pressure, helps the reluctant child to talk, may be the most helpful approach. The advocate must actively cross the boundaries the child has needed for protection, and go towards the child's inner self. This can be one of the most difficult tasks in an investigative interview. A way must be found to avoid the pitfall of giving the child so much leeway that his blocking techniques remain an insurmountable obstacle. Otherwise it may only be possible to interpret the child's play as indicative of abuse, rather than more accurately as a re-enactment of abuse, preferably leading into some spontaneous description by the child of the actual event. Many children may not achieve spontaneity in recounting their experiences until the risk of ongoing abuse is removed (Chapter 4). This can be achieved for some children in Group 2 by a short period of hospitalisation. However, affording the child a brief period of safety will not in itself be enough for some children. Since it is important for the therapeutic endeavour that the child be freed enough to share the experiences, it may be necessary to create an intimate safe space for child and advocate within this wider circle of safety. This can involve allowing the child to regress completely, or exercise total control over the immediate environment. This is described by Jan Hindmann (1987), who gives excellent help and guidance for equalising the relationship. An additional factor which the therapist must understand is that the child may later reject the interviewer; Conerly (1986,p.51) reminds us that children often get very angry with the person they tell.

One eight year old girl seemed in her drawing to represent the ideal intervention for her needs (Figure 6.3).

Figure 6.3

Her drawing depicts two giant figures, the abuser, represented in a devil mask, and the social worker, who looks quite benevolent but is of equal size. The two are engaged in conversation, with the monster saying 'I'll eat you up' and the social worker replying 'Oh no you won't'. The child is a tiny figure saying 'help'. An equally diminutive figure is descending to the child's level by climbing down the social worker's leg, saying 'I'm coming'. This is the psychologist. Somehow the therapist had managed to achieve parity with the child, who talked explicitly about long-term penetrative abuse by her stepfather. At the time, she was living at home but the stepfather had left. We suggest that the effective combination of 'powerful' social worker,and child-focused therapist was central in this case. This could stand as a model for future team-work. The therapist who can reach and enter the child's inner world certainly needs the umbrella of the child protection agency.

Conclusion

Disclosure of sexual abuse must be regarded as a process rather than an event. Sexual abuse is about a relationship, the context of which will determine whether and how the child comes to bring the abusive experience to light. Some children decide for themselves to tell an adult who can intervene, or alert someone inadvertently (group 1). A second group can be helped by active intervention to do this sooner than they might if left without help, but group 3 children are likely to remain so enmeshed in the abuse that, unable to tell, they depend on adults to act for them. This may be through the medical 'window' described in Chapter 3. Any plan for intervention should rest on the understanding that children move in either direction along the continuum (Chapter 5), sometimes towards disclosure but sometimes towards silence or denial. Children in group 2 who can be facilitated to disclose are still at risk of being trapped by moving to group 3 unless the intervention protects them from the pressures for silencing. For group 3 children, moving up the continuum is a monumental task, but they can, in certain circumstances, accomplish it, although often over a longer time-scale than the formal investigation affords. Since the needs of a silent child are easily overlooked, the advocate's central task is to keep the child at the forefront of the minds of all involved.

7 The Unwanted Message:
Child Protection Through Community Awareness
Hilary Cashman and Annette Lamballe-Armstrong

Child sexual abuse will continue as long as we simply focus on individual children, one at a time, applying crisis measures when abuse is revealed. It is also important, but not enough, that children and families and offenders are healed after sexual abuse happens. A more general healing of society is required to change attitudes which promote and condone sexually abusive behaviours. (Bagley and King, 1990)

Introduction

This chapter examines the necessity for community involvement in the prevention and healing of child sexual abuse. We suggest ways in which professionals and the community can start working together for the sake of children at risk. We uncover the influences and processes which dissuade the community from giving a mandate to professionals to protect and help children, and the catastrophic consequences.

The chapter refers to the experience of a community group, Cleveland Against Child Abuse (CAUSE). It is not intended as a history of CAUSE or the 'Cleveland crisis,' but will examine the tasks facing the pro-child community group in the light of CAUSE's experience.

CAUSE's work is unfunded. Its methods are empirical, and it works to long-term goals which cannot yet be evaluated. Short-term progress has been made by relatively simple measures: opening up the public debate about child sexual abuse, publishing basic information about abuse, telling the truth and reiterating it patiently, listening to community opinion and creating a vehicle for its expression.

Whatever the methods adopted, society must be involved in combating

119

child sexual abuse, as Pigot (1989, p. 9) makes clear, 'In this report we are concerned with aspects of the law which, in a democracy, cannot safely be left to politicians and lawyers alone. Members of the general public have a deep, significant and legitimate interest in these questions'.

Defining aims

Imagine a society which cared enough about its children to protect them from sexual abuse. In that society, children would be respected, loved and nurtured, and taught that their bodies belong to them and are not for adult gratification. Adults at risk of becoming perpetrators would be encouraged to seek confidential and freely available help, with necessary safeguards for vulnerable children. Sexual abuse would be discussed, and children given appropriate education. If any adult tempted to abuse did break through this barrier of social watchfulness, he or she would encounter a confident refusal from any potential victim. At worst, if the victim were over-powered, that child would understand the need to seek help, and know how to do so. Protective adults would take responsibility on behalf of children too young to seek help for themselves. The elements of a child-protective society therefore include awareness of the problem, provision of help for abusers or potential abusers, and the encouragement of assertiveness in children, together with universal respect for their physical and spiritual integrity. We paint this utopian picture not because the key to it is readily at hand but as a reminder that all childcare workers should try to achieve 'primary prevention' (Bagley and King, 1990, p. 207): that is, the child-loving society. Because this distant goal seems unattainable, it is easy to get stuck and waste energy accommodating to obstacles and accepting compromises.

Compare another major child heath problem. Globally, millions of children die each year from malnutrition. Like child sexual abuse, this is not a mysterious and puzzling condition. The treatment is known , and resources exist to treat it (Hayter, 1981, pp. 57–58). There is potentially enough food for the world. Child-starvation continues because the international economic order functions to withhold food from those who need it. This is tragic, but at least those trying to deal with the problem of child-starvation understand it. While working on 'first-aid' measures, the agencies also question and criticise the structures which cause starvation. The magnitude of the challenge, to change the heart of whole societies, so that children need not starve, is awesome, but it is still undertaken. The imperative of every dead or stunted child spurs health-workers on to challenge the system.

Child sexual abuse should be looked upon in the same way. Prevalence surveys (Glaser and Frosh, 1988, pp. 9-12) indicate that it is endemic in society, rather than being an occasional aberration. It is hard to prevent because this entails changing the way society regards children, families, relationships and sexuality. This task invites despair; the temptation must be resisted. Although abuse is endemic we should not be deterred from trying to help individual children effectively while at the same time playing our part in the parallel task of making the whole of society safer and more nurturing for its children.

The protective society described above is an ambitious, seemingly remote ideal. It could not be built into local or national policy, or appear on a political manifesto except as an aspiration. Nevertheless it is right that governments and parties should commit themselves to working towards the ideal:

> . . . a programme which encompasses the rights of the child essentially is a positive one. It recognises the value of every child, and seeks to bring about a social and economic environment within which each child can develop its potential. Our ultimate aim must be the creation of self-fulfilled and caring members of the community, able and willing to make a beneficial contribution to society. (Lestor 1990,p. 12).

The components of the child-loving society have to be sought far and wide. In Cleveland, as elsewhere, opportunities have presented themselves to work towards the ideal, and some of these have been taken up by CAUSE.

Developing a model

The first difficulty facing any community initiative against child sexual abuse is the lack of a suitable model. Two related social problems on which progress has been made in recent decades offer possibilities: domestic violence, and child physical abuse. Victims of domestic violence rebelled, found a voice and began to build up their strength in the context of the women's refuge movement. Neither battered nor sexually abused children had the same possibilities of self-help or communal action. However, publicity about visible injuries and occasional violent deaths eventually prompted adults to intervene on behalf of battered children. Society was shocked into learning the truth about baby-battering, and has developed a mature response to it. Sexually abused children usually show no visible injuries alarming enough to elicit adult intervention. Thus not only do they fail to get help as individuals, but also society fails to learn the necessary lessons about the occurrence of sexual abuse. The self-help model, then, is not available to child victims of sexual abuse. What other groups or individuals could speak on their behalf, and how could they do it?

Avoiding the Problem

Recent years have seen a growing interest in child sexual abuse. Incest survivors have at last been heard and the value of their contribution has been recognised. Professional practice has been developed, researched and refined. Yet a dark, unmentionable presence looms threateningly behind each new publication, at each conference: the prohibition on putting this knowledge into practice. The time is not yet ripe, runs the orthodoxy; society is not ready, the process is too traumatic.

Closer examination of this shifting of blame onto societal rejection of the problem reveals a tangle of themes. Some are rather sinister: for instance, that children's right to intervention to stop abuse must be limited by the availability of resources. The unavoidable pain when sexual abuse is revealed may also be transformed into societal refusal to acknowledge such abuse:

> . . . there is certain pain in discovery and humiliation in full disclosure. Anyone who tries to encourage unwanted awareness becomes a target for censure. . . Unlike ordinary frontiers of discovery, sexual abuse provokes an authoritarian insistence for obscurity over enlightenment. (Summit, 1988, p.45).

Political power is derived from and held by adults, and there are intractable political problems in trying to achieve priority for children's needs. Politicians may feel impelled to deny the magnitude of the problem with more determination than other groups, because they depend for their position on the support of vocal, influential adult lobbies.

Whatever the reasons for avoiding the problem, the result is that any serious attempt to address it is aborted in a 'crisis.' A few heads roll, parental rights are indignantly asserted, and professionals are left pondering the meaning of the crisis, what caused it, how it affects policy, whether it can somehow be bypassed or whether it must delay progress for a few more years. Textbooks are revised, professionals given incompatible messages. They should act to protect children, but not if the community will not allow it. They should work to develop good practice, but jettison it if sufficient political pressure is brought to bear on them. Child protection is the art of the possible. Professionals seem to be required to gamble on the consequences of helping children: a situation which threatens and disables them, and endangers children. Any practice handbook which does not admit the reality of these depressing messages is avoiding the central issues of child protection.

Each crisis is portrayed as a unique aberration, but in fact crises occur quite often, and have a cumulative effect. Summit gives several recent examples, pointing out one powerful consequence: the development of a well-organised, lucrative defence apparatus, not for children but for adults accused of abuse:

> Defense attorneys invented a theory that blames the interviewer for creating false allegations: The hapless defendants are the victims of an unhealthy alliance of prosecutors, therapists and hysterical parents whose leading questions have subliminally cued naive children into believing they were abused. . . . Expert opinions can be hired to dignify the same argument for the defence of any accused adult. (Summit 1988, p. 44).

Thus each crisis not only deters the adults who should be helping children, but strengthens the legal and societal immunity of the abuser. Is this what the community really wants? If not, how can it arrive at a more child-friendly consensus and see it put into practice?

We suggest the following four-stage process as a model of how the need for advocacy for abused children may become apparent, and effective advocacy can be developed:

Stage I.   Knowledge of child sexual abuse is largely hidden from the public gaze, and confined to the professional domain. There is no social context in which a broad lobby to help abused children can develop.

Stage II.   The hidden problem erupts in crisis, overwhelming the professionals and spilling out into the community. It is at this stage that the lack of effective advocacy for abused children becomes catastrophic. The group we might naturally look to for such advocacy, child-care professionals, faces various obstacles. Some may have unthinkingly adopted theories inimical to children's well-being, and therefore have no base from which to speak for children without losing face. Without a societal mandate to deal with the problem, some may be compromised in respect of their own practice. In Cleveland, for instance, local paediatricians seemed to have almost ceased to diagnose child sexual abuse by early 1989, except in cases where the concern had been raised by someone else. One suggested explanation was that local child-molesters had developed their technique so as not to leave physical signs. Whatever one makes of this extraordinary suggestion, it seems that professional beliefs about child sexual abuse remain polarised. The few professionals who are willing to speak on behalf of children, and give accurate and frank information, may be under threat or already victimised for taking child sexual abuse seriously, and their contributions may be dismissed as self-justifying. They cannot use the most telling information of all – confidential clinical evidence about individual children, which would enable the community to understand what really happened.

The most knowledgeable group about child sexual abuse (apart from its perpetrators) is abuse survivors. They know the forms it takes, the damage it does and the difficulty of healing. They too, however, can be dismissed as being partisan and lacking objectivity. The respect often accorded to self-help and community groups is denied to them, and excuses are found to marginalise them (Kitzinger, 1989). Indeed, the worse the abuse suffered, the easier it may be to dismiss a survivor as too damaged to contribute to the discussion. This is one way in which society perpetuates child sexual abuse and carries on the abuser's work. Survivors' groups, then, are permitted to provide counselling and sup-port to other adult survivors; but they are not consulted or heeded when they speak on behalf of children currently being sexually ex-ploited.

The mass media might be expected to consider advocacy for children as a public duty, but they too tend to fail children at this stage of the process. A local paper in Cleveland showed where its priorities lay by using a running slogan 'Give us back our children'. The media cam-paign rarely attempted to balance the voices of angry adults with some

124

responsible background information on child sexual abuse, and became 'a debacle compounded by sloppy, sensationalist journalism' (Illsley, 1990).

This failure of formal systems to produce a child-centred resolution to the crisis eventually pushed ordinary people in Cleveland into creating their own initiative. They had waited for several months for 'the system' to right itself, set the record straight and create better services for children. They had watched with increasing incredulity and dismay as the recommendations of the Butler-Sloss report were ignored, conscientious professionals were scapegoated, and children's welfare stayed at the bottom of the agenda. Public anger at this state of affairs moved the process on to the next stage.

Stage III   At this stage the community begins to understand that it must act independently to create its own vehicle for change. With children silenced and survivors and professionals ignored, it becomes clear that other voices are needed. Community groups with a core of non-abused and non-abusing adults, in alliance with survivors, principled professionals and any others prepared to help, are well-placed to initiate the process of discussion and education. In Cleveland, ordinary people at last began to address the chaos and conflict of the crisis, and taking the problem into their own hands held the first public meeting about child sexual abuse. CAUSE developed from the realisation by individuals and groups worried about the adult-centred political settlement of the crisis that they were not alone. Despair at the failure of the authorities to address the problem lent urgency to the group's meetings. Initial dismay gave way to determination to achieve priority for children.

The community group has many potential allies, and it is important not to have rigid ideas of which groups will be helpful and which not. In one area the Rape Crisis Centre may play a leading role; in another it may be compromised by the need to secure funding. In one area police-surgeons may be unskilled and obstructive in abuse work; in another, police doctors such as the Northumbria Women Police Doctors Group may take the initiative in developing local services. In all areas, the people most qualified to help abused children are those with children's welfare most at heart, whatever their position or formal qualifications.

A broad coalition to help abused children therefore starts from a tripartite alliance of abuse survivors, conscientious professionals and concerned community members. Some individuals may be in more than one category.

Around the time of a child-abuse 'crisis', membership of such a coalition may be affected by restrictions. For a long time it was dangerous or impossible for anyone employed by the County Council or the Health Authority in Cleveland to speak publicly about child sexual abuse or be openly associated with CAUSE. These bans were enforced by both formal prohibition and pressure and intimidation. In May 1989 staff and elected members of Cleveland County Council were banned from speaking in public about child abuse. The paradoxical situation thus arose that Sue Richardson, one of Britain's most experienced and highly trained social work practitioners in the area of child sexual abuse, was not allowed to share in the task of raising public awareness about abuse, but remained silenced and isolated by her employers.

Stage IV. Once the community group is established, specific tasks emerge: informing the community, questioning popular myths, resetting the agenda to focus on children, offering support to professionals committed to children, consulting the community and demanding attention for community views. The group must start by educating itself thoroughly about the problem, possible responses to it, and obstacles to dealing with it. The next stage – passing the knowledge on, so that an informed public debate can take place – is difficult and daunting. In Cleveland this meant breaking the silence which had fallen on the community since 1987. Questioning the orthodoxy – that the professionals had made massive mistakes in 1987, disclosing imaginary abuse and tearing 'innocent families' apart – was unpopular and difficult even in private conversation. Many people had doubts about the media portrayal of events, but felt isolated and fearful. Once CAUSE existed as a visible alternative to the political and media consensus, it became a focus for open and honest discussion. The resulting interest and concern were denounced as reopening old wounds by local health and social services managers, whose policy of silence and self-censorship was based on an irreconcilably different approach. Ignoring official disapproval, the group set up a series of meetings on such topics as: support for mothers of abused children, teachers' role in child-protection, options for dealing with abusers, ways of surviving abuse and repairing the damage.

To build a broad base, the pro-child group must catch people's attention and arouse their interest. This process, in Cleveland, was partly involuntary. CAUSE was challenged on its attitude to the professionals scapegoated after the Cleveland crisis and took a considered decision to support them. This was incorporated in the CAUSE constitution. We took the view, later proved correct, that a disastrous consequence of victimisation would be that other professionals would be deterred from helping abused children (Evening Gazette, 1st April 1990). This support was not given unconditionally; it was based on a close examination of their work with children. For supporting the professionals, CAUSE was attacked and smeared by local politicians and media. The main thrust of our work on community education was for a long time ignored. Yet our stand, forced into prominence by these challenges and attacks, did provoke discussion and sow seeds of doubt about the popular picture of the crisis.

Once the discussion began, this picture began to be examined and questioned. It seemed that the portrayal of events in the media had led to the creation of well-defined 'myths' which fuelled anxieties in people's minds about what might have happened. These myths were corrected in a short leaflet, 'Fifteen myths about child sexual abuse and Cleveland' (see Appendix A). This leaflet has proved valuable, both for its information content and as a way of questioning assumptions about child sexual abuse. Once people identified points on which they had been misled, they were prepared to question other myths and face other depressing facts: that abuse can occur in loving and 'normal' families; that it can take place in foster homes; that babies are abused.

As we later discovered, others (e.g. Driver, 1989) have used the same approach of confronting and refuting the myriad myths surrounding child sexual abuse, such as that chidren invite abuse, or that sexual abuse is commoner in working-class families. The persistence of the myths in the face of comprehensive refutations suggests that mere factual correction is not enough. The myths seem to have their own self-perpetuating energy, and function to minimise and deny child sexual abuse. Attempts at refutation must be strengthened with a similar energy and determination. This was the aim of CAUSE's widespread distribution of our leaflet. The myths are used to construct an impenetrable defensive wall around child-molesters; shock-tactics, as well as patient dismantling, may be needed to break it down.

Another indispensable element of community learning is a dialogue between lay people and professionals. In Cleveland this evolved during the early work of CAUSE. In developing our own knowledge about child sexual abuse, we confronted the professionals involved in the crisis with many challenges, queries and doubts, all of which were answered comprehensively and patiently. We were impressed by their response, and set up further meetings with women's groups, church groups, trade unions, teachers and others, to carry on the learning process.

We began to realise that this process, rather than being an arduous task of setting the record straight, represented the beginnings of the professional/community alliance for which we were striving: the key to constructing the community mandate for professionals to do child-abuse work. In such an alliance, professionals are willingly accountable to the communities they serve, learning to explain and discuss their work, and in turn relying upon community support for it. This is absolutely essential in child-abuse work and would be a model of good practice throughout the caring professions.

In beginning this dialogue, we had stumbled upon the way forward and started to put it into practice. This became a permanent feature of CAUSE's work, with a high level of commitment and willingness from those involved. In Cleveland, any group can be provided by CAUSE with a range of speakers. This kind of dialogue breaks down barriers between professional and lay people, between specialist and everyday language. Lay people may have to overcome mistrust of professionals. Professionals have to learn to manage without technical shorthand and explain their work clearly. Traditional hierarchies are set aside, although each participant's skills are acknowledged and respected, the better for being understood. As Madara (1987, p. 29) points out: 'In negotiating any partnership, a true sense of equality and mutual respect for each other's values and knowledge is needed, whether it be experiential or professional knowledge.'

A group that develops this method has the potential to become a strong and effective pro-child coalition, able to make authoritative statements on behalf of children's interests. Different members will be appropriate spokespeople in different situations. The pro-child alliance, cutting across traditional roles, can be flexible, resourceful and task-oriented, drawing on formal or informal skills. It is well-equipped to develop its most essential skill, communication between disparate groups. It may be compared with groups such as Parents United in California (Giarretto,1982), which similarly draws on a community/professional alliance to heal child sexual abuse. CAUSE's brief is different, in that it is not a service provider but aims at bringing about prevention and healing by social change; and it is a pressure group based on the whole community of non-abusing adults and survivors, rather than a mutual help group of people sharing the same painful experiences. However, it derives its strength from similar sources; recognition of the community as a key resource and readiness to cross boundaries in order to bring about change.

Taking responsibility

The process of learning, discussion and information sharing in stage 4 should lead to society's accepting its share of responsibility for child protection. For example, CAUSE's work of examining the myths in public meetings or small groups, led participants to face up to the real tasks of child protection, previously regarded as too complex for lay people to consider. Challenged by Campbell's (1988, p.4) succinct question 'What would *you* have done?', we confronted such dilemmas as 'What do you do if a young girl has left home because of sexual abuse by her stepfather, but her two-year-old brother is still at home?', 'What do you do think should happen if a toddler shows abnormal anal signs which resolve after several days in hospital?', 'What can you do if an abused child wants to stay at home but his parents do not believe he could possibly have been abused, and therefore are unable to protect him?' Groups considering these dilemmas gradually respond positively to Butler-Sloss's comment (Butler-Sloss, 1988, p. 245): 'Social workers need the support of the public to continue in the job the public needs them to do.' Such discussion must be well-informed and rigorous. It is possible to debate child sexual abuse inconclu-sively, using assumptions or anecdotes to support one's favoured position. It is only possible to move to a constructive discussion by careful consideration of accurate data.

Becoming a voice for the community

The group must assess and honestly represent community feeling. One dilemma it may face is what support to offer professionals victimised for protecting children. Does the community understand this support, or might it be seen as damaging to the group's independence and objectivity? These themes came together in CAUSE's first year in a project which changed our perspective radically and pointed to possibilities for progress. We carried out a carefully structured, large scale door to door survey in South Cleveland, asking people's opinions about child sexual abuse in general and inviting their support for one of the paediatricians, Dr. Higgs, whose future was under threat.

We did not know what response to expect. The professionals had been so vilified in Cleveland that it seemed impossible that people would judge the issues calmly, yet they did. Most expressed concern about sexual abuse. Many asked for further information about abuse and about the events of 1987. Many spoke with disgust of the public figures who had made political capital out of children's suffering. 62 percent of those we approached signed a petition on behalf of the paediatrician . 25 percent said they needed more information before signing. Only 9 percent refused categorically. This survey challenged supposedly massive public consensus against Dr. Higgs, and gave us information with implications far beyond her individual legal situation. It showed that ordinary people in Cleveland had a level of concern about child sexual abuse which had stubbornly survived a concerted , often vicious media campaign; that they were ready to talk about the problems and eager for accurate, unbiased information. If this is true for Cleveland, it is reasonable to assume that it is true elsewhere. CAUSE's agenda was transformed by this exercise. We realised that, instead of labouring to raise awareness in an apathetic community, we were the voice of a community already concerned about the protection of children. Our task now was to demand attention for that long-ignored community feeling. A particular focus needed to be those designated as community representatives, who instead voiced their own prejudices .

Once there is a sufficient level of public concern, the group's next step is to explore opportunities for general information-sharing and discussion. After publishing our survey results, CAUSE arranged a public meeting on health aspects of child sexual abuse, addressed by the two paediatricians involved in the crisis and introduced by a local MP. This well-attended meeting was not only a useful discussion; it symbolically broke the isolation of both paediatricians by the community.

CAUSE's role in bringing about open discussion, and expressing an alternative to the powerful political consensus, thus enabled others to speak out on behalf of children. Eventually the more intractable problems must be addressed, for instance the Catch 22 by which professionals are discouraged from revealing sexual abuse if resources are not available to deal with it properly, while resources cannot be made available as long as the problem stays hidden. The political task of mobilising resources belongs to the community and will be undertaken by the community, once there is understanding of the damage and devastation wrought by child sexual abuse.

A range of interwoven problems must be understood to address this task. It is no good educating teachers to be sensitive and competent in picking up abuse if social workers cannot provide back-up. Social work expertise cannot help the child if the police abdicate their investigative role. Skilled police work will not benefit the victim if the legal system then fails that child. All workers committed to children's welfare need and deserve the understanding and support of their community.

Making the voice louder

The community has a right and duty to make demands on behalf of its children. The people of Cleveland were portrayed during the crisis as more interested in parents' rights than children's welfare; and communities in general are portrayed, in this context, as apathetic, uninterested, a hindrance to progress. CAUSE discovered instead that ordinary people are worried about child abuse and ready to make resources available to treat it. The next step is to make that community opinion bold, assertive and insistent in demanding good services for children and families. We should make our opinions and wishes known to relevant agencies, including:

– *legal bodies and the police*. The legal system, formed by adults, is weighted heavily against children, yet there is potential which can be developed to help children. The Criminal Injuries Compensation Board can give a public demonstration of an abuse victim's right to compensation, which emphasises the serious nature of the crime. An energetic and proactive Crown Prosecution Service can explore ways of bringing a prosecution even where the child is very young. The police may become frustrated at the limits of their ability to help children, especially when a prosecution cannot be brought. At worst, the prosecution mentality can lead to the police 'losing sight of their wider responsibilities for the interests and welfare of the children involved.' (Butler-Sloss, 1988, p.100). The community can only understand the police role, its value and limitations, if there is genuine consultation and accountability;

– *the clergy:* an influential element in the local community, but often prone to express an uninformed, knee-jerk, 'families first' reaction which ignores the child's pain. In the United States the churches have produced more initiatives and a more thoughtful approach to abuse, possibly because there are more female clergy in US churches (Briggs, 1990);

– *pressure groups representing adults' interests.* Some voluntary groups conflate the rights of adults and children into the idea of 'family rights,' camouflaging the fact that the two may be incompatible. The family rights rallying call can be used by groups and individuals to further the maintenance of parental control whatever the cost to the child

– *Members of Parliament.* The problem must be addressed at parliamentary level. There are signs of a coherent approach beginning to develop. One British political party now has a shadow Minister for Children, prepared to take child abuse seriously (Lestor, 1990). Two Cleveland MPs have given CAUSE consistent support. The legislative situation, however, gives little cause for optimism. As Wattam et al (1989, p.64) pointed out:

> Recent reforms reflect political ambivalence about helping children . . . [the Children Act 1989] seems to be more concerned with limiting professionals' legal powers and increasing parental rights than with improving services for families and children;

– *local government and health service management.* Community groups should be represented on local bodies dealing with child protection, where they can channel grassroots information and opinion to the authorities and if necessary challenge assumptions made by political and professional representatives. They may also press for children's needs to be given a higher profile, for instance by the appointment of a Children's Rights Officer or the establishment of a Children's Bureau.

If public bodies for whatever reasons fail to do all in their power to deal effectively with child sexual abuse, they give tacit permission for abuse to continue. Society has a duty to withdraw that permission.

Dealing with conflict

The pro-child coalition must expect to encounter strong opposition. This is the universal experience of advocates for children. As Alice Miller (1986, pp 18-19) discovered 'Those who take a stand in today's world on behalf of workers, women or even mistreated animals will find a group to represent them, but someone who becomes a strong advocate for the child . . . will stand alone.' Abused children are largely powerless. Abusers are in a powerful position and unlikely to accept any threat to their freedom to use children sexually. CAUSE was criticised from its inception for creating conflict in a community which was wrongly perceived as calm and united. However, we accept that child sexual abuse is a constant feature of our society, usually remaining hidden and undisclosed. It must also be apparent that any attempt to challenge this situation will elicit a violent opposition and result in unavoidable conflict. The community group should perhaps expect personal attacks and smears. It should be tactful, reflective and strategic, remaining centred on its task by keeping children's well-being at the top of its agenda. Conflicts may also arise within the group itself. Abuse survivors, for instance, may have criticisms of professional practice. Professionals may feel misunderstood. Lay members may feel undervalued. Group members may use different kinds of language and have to struggle to understand each other. Working through genuine conflict together helps to develop mutual trust and respect.

Conclusion

The pro-child coalition should be innovative and open-minded. It has to break new ground. There will be pressures to become a service-giving rather than a campaigning group, especially as the group becomes known and is seen by the community as a referral and resource point. Individual members may be active in mothers' support groups, survivors' networks or children's charities, but the group itself should not be sidetracked into spending its energy in a hopeless attempt to meet needs which society as a whole should be challenged to recognise. Local authorities, too, may try to coopt the troublesome, demanding pressure group and turn it into a small-scale, low-cost service provider, especially at times of financial stringency. This should be resisted.

Since the power of the group derives from its main resource, individual members, it may not have a fixed ideological starting point, apart from prioritising the needs of children. Feminism, by seeing sexual abuse as a manifestation of male sexual aggression and exploitation, has informed much of the work on developing societal responses to child sexual abuse (as distinct from clinical or legal responses). CAUSE was not founded on feminist principles. It is a broadly-based alliance endeavouring to call attention to the needs of children over and above adults' rights or 'family rights.' Feminism influences some of its ideas; others derive from humanist, spiritual or other concepts of the integrity of the human person, and our collective responsibility to protect that integrity. 'Behind each statistic, there is a child. She may be you. She may be your daughter. She may be your sister. She may be your friend. You cannot protect her until we can protect all children.' (Bass and Thornton, 1983, pp. 37–8).

8 Questions Not Answers: Progressing the Debate

Sue Richardson and Heather Bacon

Halfway down the stairs
Is a stair where I sit.
There isn't any other stair
Quite like it.
I'm not at the bottom
I'm not at the top.
So this is the stair where I always stop.
(A.A.Milne, 1924)

Introduction.

The aim of this chapter is to progress the debate which we believe to be essential to generate creative responses to an intractable problem. If there are solutions, they will be found only through wider change in the political and social structure of society. We see the post-Cleveland debate as having been inhibited by lack of accurate information, narrow professional and procedural concerns, fear, and attempts to 'close down' the problem. In Cleveland, for example, this is reflected in the figures for children on the Child Protection Register, (Cleveland County Council, 1990), which recorded a drop in the year 1989-1990 of 48.4 percent in the number of children registered under the category of sexual abuse. The task of progressing the debate and ensuring a more realistic response to abused children belongs to the whole community (Chapter 7). In our experience, the debate is opened up at the initiative of survivors, either adults who have painfully reclaimed their power and energy following abuse as children, or professionals who have been victimised. Like victims of other forms of trauma, both depend on others to reach out but find that few will do so

135

unless the victims themselves break the taboo on speaking of their experiences. Enlightened colleagues and lay members of the community play a key role in facilitating this process. However, their experience cannot extend beyond a certain point: they have not 'been there'. Difficulties in communication can open up and there can be differences in understanding from each perspective.

The need to contain the problem of child abuse within manageable limits and avoid challenging the social structure of the family has produced a 'new orthodoxy', in which the emphasis has been on adult consensus at the expense of children's interests. Where adult and child interests conflict irreconcilably, the dilemmas of case management have remained un-addressed. We argue that if children are to be protected there is no neutral position to be taken: our response should be based on unequivocal advocacy for the child. This involves breaking an unwritten rule that the professional should remain detached from the family system, keeping an overview rather than taking sides. We agree with Margolin's view (1982), that the responsibility for the consequences of intervention rests most heavily with respect to the interests of future generations. In this chapter we explore a new perspective on what might be seen as a 'successful outcome' and address the issue of professional survival and victimisation.

Towards a Successful Outcome

We hold that a successful outcome should be defined in terms of the quality of the intervention rather than the success or failure of the whole enterprise, or whether procedures were rigidly adhered to. We believe that conflicts of interest should be resolved by allowing the interests of the child to take precedence over the welfare of the family or of other individuals. The child should not have to put up with continuing abuse in order to keep a family together. Many children remain in their families, subject to ongoing abuse, despite the best efforts of child protection agencies. Such practice decisions are inextricably bound up with underlying ideologies. There is an unresolved argument about whether sexual abuse is the result of a particular pattern of relationships – the dysfunctional family – or the result of individual pathology (Kidd and Pringle 1988).

Ideally, successful intervention would detect and prevent abuse without being at the expense of the child who risks being unable to live with the family,or the perpetrator who is frequently punished and not helped. A successful outcome ideally requires that neither child nor perpetrator remain trapped in damaging cycles of abuse. In the absence of enough resources for therapy and good quality substitute care, there are valid concerns about 'secondary victimisation' by the system (Pigot, 1989). While we agree with Harrop (1990, p.11) that we must aim to 'show children that there might be another way of living that does not depend on being sexually abused ', we have difficulty with his contention that 'If we patently fail to achieve this aim, . . . we need the honesty to choose between our abuse and the probability of further abuse within the family should the child return home.' If the care the family gives includes abuse, which cannot be addressed jointly in work with them, the solution lies in providing better alternative care for the child. In other words, if the system abuses the child, the system needs to change: the child should not have to pay while we avoid this responsibility. Equally, our knowledge that the system is less than perfect should not lead us to avoid our responsibility to intervene.

We recognise the validity of the stance that any therapeutic effort directed towards the perpetrator is child protection work. Perpetrators are often trapped in patterns of thinking which rationalise and deny the meaning of their acts for the victim. Lindblad (1990) questions the assumption that few perpetrators make a confession, finding that 8 out of 19 accused of intrafamilial abuse were able to confirm what the child had said. More effective interviewing techniques for suspected abusers may help some to confirm the allegations. By helping children to talk and making their statements available, we may provide better ways to confront perpetrators with what happened. A note of caution here is that if the investigation still fails, the child whose confidentiality has been broken may be in danger.

The best chance to protect children while at the same time ensuring a therapeutic attitude to families may be to combine statutory authority (Chapter 2) to control the perpetrator, with support for the non–abusing caretaker and treatment for the child. This requires that child advocates accept involvement with the legal system and communicate with the wider social system. Work is needed to show the effectiveness of this type of approach, exemplified by the comprehensive treatment programme developed by Giaretto (1981) which mobilises resources in the community particularly mothers and perpetrators who have already been through the programme. This allows for professional accountability and also for responsibility to be taken by the community. However, the effectiveness of this humanistic family-centred approach has been questioned as more knowledge has emerged about perpetrator's behaviour. Different programmes have different outcomes according to their philosophies. Toller (1989) comments that there is little comparative information available about the relative success of different treatments.

Public opinion in Cleveland held that families where abuse had not occurred were abused by the system. Several experts to the inquiry expressed concern that a lowered threshold for investigation would catch up an unacceptably high proportion of innocent families. We feel that healthy families can survive child abuse investigations, provided they are given support, especially to deal with practical disruptions and emotional reactions, including anger. It may be hard to disentangle the reactions of families where abuse is occurring from the reaction of a family where it is not. However, if the assessment of the child's position is given priority (Chapter 6) this will provide the clearest picture of the true situation. On balance we feel that a lowered threshold for concern and investigation is necessary. Otherwise abuse has to be staring us in the face before procedures can be invoked.

It is easy to agree that whatever is done should be child-centred; defining this is more difficult but not impossible. The pitfall of multi-agency co-operation is that this may become an end in itself and not the means whereby the child can be held at the forefront of everyone's mind. Valuable learning and debate are to be found in the inquiry report. We learned many lessons as professionals striving, and sometimes failing, to get it right. The difficulties are affirmed by Butler-Sloss in her conclusion:

It is difficult for professionals to balance the conflicting interests and needs in the enormously important and delicate field of child sexual abuse. We hope that professionals will not as a result of the Cleveland experience stand back and hesitate to act to protect the children' (Butler-Sloss, 1988, p.244.)

Models For a Child-Centred Approach.

In Cleveland (Butler-Sloss 1988, p. 209) we were said to view the child's disclosure as 'the gold standard' in the detection of sexual abuse. However, since many children cannot disclose, it is essential that in future children can be afforded protection on the evidence of a medical diagnosis alone.

138

This would help many children who remain trapped. In addition, as much as possible must be done to enable children to talk of abusive experiences. All child advocates will be familiar with the way children move up and down the continuum once abuse starts coming to light. In order to respond sensitively to the child's needs at any point this dynamic must firstly be accepted and understood.

Creative, child-centred, well-researched ways are needed to help child victims unlock their secret during investigations. These must be combined with greater acceptance in the legal system for these approaches so that children's testimony is less readily dismissed. There is an encouraging body of evidence that children can and should be regarded as competent witnesses, which is leading to serious consideration of how the legal system can be made less traumatising for them. (e.g.Davies and Flynn, 1988). Pigot (1989) recommends that for some children, their trusted advocate, who could be a doctor, nurse, teacher, or health worker, should be allowed to participate in the initial joint investigation and conduct the interview provided they are properly instructed. Butler-Sloss (1988, p. 249) recommended specialist assessment teams who can be brought in at any stage in the investigation where difficulty is anticipated. We agree with Appleyard (1990, p. 46) who felt that 'members of the specialist team should have some continuing responsibility for the decisions that they make'. Such measures could create the opportunity for a child-centred approach right from the start. However we must remember that what the child says may be an unreliable indicator of what has actually happened, not because children invent stories but because many will deny or minimise abuse. The concept of the continuum of disclosure can be helpful in planning any investigation. Ways of matching the type of interview to the child's position are suggested in Chapter 6. The central dilemma for abused children who have not already disclosed is how to move them up the continuum within the timescale of the investigation. The 'watching brief' is one way to approach this task (Butler-Sloss, 1988 p.249). Nothing is done to intervene directly to protect the child, but support and the availability of an advocate may nevertheless help the child to tell about ongoing abuse. A flexible model for intervention which includes this option has been described by Coates et.al.(1990) and is represented in figure 8.1.

We emphasise the need to reconsider decisions to prevent 'stuckness', especially endless circling round in the 'watching brief' option. We feel the watching brief alternative has a limited chance of success for children who

Making Decisions about levels of intervention

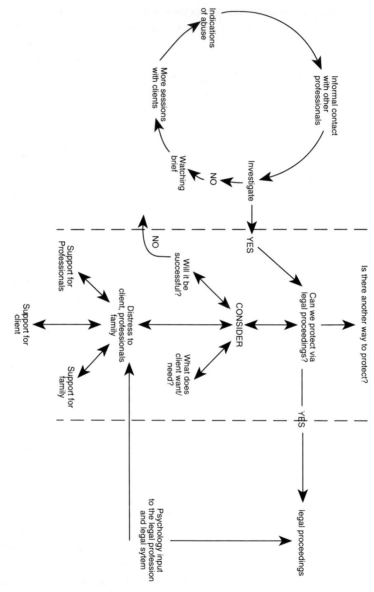

Figure 8

have become very accommodated to long term abuse. It can be tried as an option for those who are assessed as beginning to mobilise their own resistance, perhaps because they recognise that the abuse is wrong and harmful.

Removal From Home : A Key Dilemma.

Butler-Sloss (1988 p.7.) noted a key dilemma: 'The idea would be to protect the child within his or her home and neighbourhood, preferably after identifying and excluding the abuser. However, if, as is often the case, the perpetrator is unknown, or is suspected but denies the abuse, how can the child be protected?' There are powers under Section 1 of the 1980 Act which social services could use to defray costs for a suspected abuser leaving home while an initial assessment is completed (Butler-Sloss, 1988 p. 254). Also according to Butler-Sloss, (1990, p.76) 'it may at times very briefly be appropriate to keep the child apart' during initial investigation.

A debate on the issues surrounding whether children should be separated from the family during the diagnostic phase predates the Cleveland crisis.

Bentovim (1987, p. 37) writing on the importance of diagnosing child sexual abuse describes two over-riding concerns, 'to ensure that the child is protected from further abuse and to prevent long-term effects and define the most effective ways of treatment for the family'. He cites several dilemmas for clinicians in interviewing children, including the resistance demonstrated by some children to describing experiences even in the presence of physical findings, the inability of perpetrators to face the truth of their actions, so that confronting the parents produces a crisis which prevents a proper assessment of the child's needs, and the ethical issues of reporting abuse when this may lead to destructive effects for the family.

Bentovim (1987, p. 41) comments that flexible solutions must be found for these problems but points out that 'in a context where silence is demanded, the child is left dangerously exposed'. Justice Waite (1986) delivered a judgement in which he commented on the difficulty of making a diagnosis by interviewing: 'For the sake of ensuring a genuine and spontaneous response from the child, the parents should be kept in ignorance as to the real purpose of the inquiry. An element of suppressed truth, sometimes even of a deception, therefore becomes inevitable'.

Taking this further, Levental (1987, p. 32) discusses the decision made by a doctor as to whether to tell parents of concerns arising from a medical examination rather than from a complaint by the child. He suggests that if the doctor is worried that the parent is involved in the abuse, the details be withheld until an opportunity is created for the child to be seen separately. The conditions for allowing a child home when there is a strong suspicion of abuse are that 'the mother seems to believe the child and understand the concerns and the child will not be living with the alleged abuser until the matter is resolved'. There are also 'highly dangerous' risks involved in letting a child who has disclosed go home, such as threatening leading to silencing, continuing sexual abuse, and physical abuse for revealing the secret. He concludes that the decision to allow a child to go home should be made jointly between doctor and social worker and should depend on the certainty of the diagnosis, the safety of the current living arrangements, and the ability of the parent to support the child.

These recommendations seem to us to have represented the 'state of the art' prior to the Cleveland crisis. The implications of acting on them had perhaps not been widely tested in clinical situations. The furore which surrounded decision-making in Cleveland when abuse was diagnosed led to questioning of the need to remove children from home. Stevenson (1990) says that there was an apparently uncritically accepted belief that the damage of leaving children at home when there was strong suspicion outweighed the damage which might be done by immediate removal and subsequent experiences in hospital or elsewhere. She comments that the decision to remove may not have been the outcome of measured professional assessment of the risks to the particular child of being left at home. This begs the question of how this is to be done. Jaudes and Morris (1990) point out that the decision to remove from home 'may not always be made with reference to the severity of the child's medical and personal risk, even when the perpetrator has access to the child at home'. This study showed that unless there is an initial history or disclosure of abuse, the child is unlikely to be removed from home.

We found that it is sometimes difficult to carry out a measured professional assessment in the context of an outpatient clinic once parents have been alerted to the concerns. We accept that there cannot be a blanket approach to action in this situation. Rapid decision making is sometimes called for even whilst in the consulting room (Chapter 4). The only way to protect the child during what is likely to become a crisis for the family, and to plan for proper assessment, may be to admit the child to hospital and if necessary to impose restrictions on the freedom of parents to prevent this.

Mothers: Myth and Reality

We have emphasised throughout the book that the context of the abusive relationship is all-important in understanding the effects on the child both of the abuse and of disclosure. We stress the needs of the child for an advocate within the family. We have learned from Cleveland that the mother's response is one of the key elements in how the child will cope with the pressures to move up and down the continuum of disclosure. Mothers in Cleveland did not behave in a uniform or stereotyped way. We would like to address the myth that mothers are at best irresponsible or inadequate in failing to protect their children or at worst are collusive or complicit in the abuse. In particular we did not find evidence to support Kempe's view (1978) that 'we have simply not seen an innocent mother in cases of long standing incest'. It seems more likely that, like children whose recovery from the effects of abuse depends on their developmental stage and emotional health, mothers will respond in different ways to the process of abuse coming to light. This view is supported by Salt et.al.(1990) whose study reported considerable variety in mothers' response, influenced by the quality of the mother's own relationships. Salt showed that more than 90 percent of mothers showed at least a 'moderate degree' of concern for their child, and more than 80 percent took some action to protect them. 77 percent expressed no anger towards the child. The most difficult situation for mothers to deal with was an abuser who would not leave the child's home. When asked to do so, only 22 percent of mothers could make this demand on the abuser. Another key finding is that almost half the mothers were as pre-occupied with the effects on themselves as with those on the child.

In focusing on protective mothers we do not imply that mothers cannot or do not sometimes perpetrate sexual abuse, but this was rarely the case in the group of children we saw. We do not know with any certainty what influenced the mothers in Cleveland, but we observed consistently that if the mother could hear a clear account of an abusive experience directly from the child, this was very likely to elicit a protective and supportive response. The combination of advocates for both child and mother seemed to help children over the hurdle of telling their mothers.

Mothers who were offered their own worker at a special resource centre (Chapter 2) could act more supportively towards the child and with less hostility to the professionals acting on behalf of the child. The mother's emotional dependence on the child may have been one important element for some children who wanted to protect their mothers from the consequences of their becoming able to tell. Sadly, some children accurately perceived that even with support their mother would remain unable to free them from keeping a protective silence.

This has important implications for children in Group B (Chapter 3) where the concern was not raised by a disclosure from the child. If we are to utilise the medical 'window' into sexual abuse for these children we have to be prepared for the mother's problems in accepting not what the child, but a professional is saying. In such a circumstance the mother has a great distance to move along her own 'continuum of belief'. She may not be able to do so in time with the child. This is why a temporary period of separation between mother and child is so problematic for some mothers, who need the child's actual presence to reinforce their will to put the child first. Even if the mother does not see the child, the child will have an active image of the mother, and of what she is likely in the child's mind to say or do. Separation can lead the child further away from the reality of a mother who might react differently given support. Mothers may also be influenced by the child's age. Some mothers could not contemplate that their very young children had been abused, but tended to believe and sometimes blame older children. The outcome could be very positive for younger children where the mother did believe. This dimension may be underpinned by the length of time the mother perceived as elapsing before the child reported the abuse.

Once mothers accept that their children have been abused they go through a complex grief reaction which may include guilt, self recrimination, anger and depression. As with young children, we suggest that mothers who appear to be psychologically healthier at the beginning have more inner resources to draw on, and can accept and be offered appropriate support, will be better able to gain access to and express the full range of emotions necessary for resolution of the crisis.

We ignore the needs and strengths of mothers at our peril: they are the child's best resource and without them, children can only have a second best chance to overcome the effects of sexual abuse.

Pressures on Child Advocates: The Professional Continuum

Miller (1986, pp.18-19) comments that it was not until she wrote her books about childhood suffering that she found out how hostile society is to children and how this fact is ignored. Her writings capture the difficulty of acting for children where this conflicts with prevailing societal beliefs,where the memory of the advocate's own childhood hurts may be stirred and where the advocate risks rejection. Most adults, needing not to question the emotional sacrifices they made in their own childhood, are threatened by the stand of unequivocal advocacy. Miller's views are borne out by Summit (1988, p.45) who concludes that 'unlike ordinary frontiers of discovery, sexual abuse provokes an authoritarian insistence for obscurity over enlightenment'. As a result, the task of protecting children will often have to be undertaken in a hostile or adversarial context. Surviving in order to carry out this task is as much a necessity as an act of courage, since 'At stake is the survival of one's authentic self, and in this regard there is no alternative but to try to survive' (Miller 1986, p.14).

We would define professional survival as the ability to remain child centred and committed to working with the issue of child abuse, irre-spective of the outcome for us as professionals when we may be criticised or restricted in our work. The authors have experienced maintaining this commitment in professional adversity. This has led us to understand the need for freedom as professionals to move on a continuum of our own, as shown in Figure 8.2.

Like the concept embodied in the continuum of disclosure (Chapter 5), we view professional survival as a process rather than an event. A dynamic interaction of forces can produce the potential for movement in either an adult or a child centred direction. The child's distress can motivate movement either way, depending on how the adult perceives and copes with this. The interaction of conflicting pressures means that the advocate's place on the continuum can never be static. Decisions have to made as to whether to shift position when this might lead to rapid and dramatic changes. For example, social workers at the frontiers of ritual abuse who were praised by the high court for their work in protecting children were subsequently vilified and attacked, had their work questioned, and came into dispute with their employers (Dawson et.al. 1990). There is a particularly powerful fear surrounding work in the area of ritual abuse. Hopkins (1989) has pointed out the need for staff care in the child

Professional Continuum

child centred

Acceptance of 'new orthodoxy' (taking seriously rather than believe)

advocacy on behalf of the professional's inner child – space to listen and believe and deal with own feelings

following procedures to letter

freedom to act as a child advocate

conflict avoidance

able and willing to disclose on behalf of child

restriction of professional role

job security

silencing of key individuals scapegoating threats (of legal action)

support network and shared belief system

child's distress

media bias/campaigns

ability to cope with rejection hostility etc : communication

restriction of public debate

alliance with and empowerment of survivors and non-abusing family members

powerlessness inexperience doubt lack of confidence lack of advocate for professional's inner child

mandate from community via open debate

permission to experience conflict

isolation

overcoming own denial

adult centred

Figure 8.2

protection field, and the pressures which can be exerted on individuals not to continue exposing levels of abuse which are potentially difficult for the organisation to handle. He makes comparisons with the Vietnam experience, involving estrangement from others, symptoms of post-traumatic stress and rejection from a world which does not want to hear.

In our experience, it takes time to acknowledge the reality of finding oneself in this situation. The initial perception is of being in a 'short race' (Hopkins, 1989). At this stage, which lasted for us up until the publication of the Butler-Sloss report, the assumption is that a shift in opinion is imminent as the facts become known and resources are made available. Survival is taken to be a matter of maintaining one's position in the short term while alliances are made on the basis of rational argument. As events begin to stretch without resolution over a longer period, the realisation gradually dawns that the race has turned 'into a marathon' in which 'it requires stamina and commitment just to keep going'(Hopkins, 1989, p.17.). By this stage, individual room for manoeuvre is likely to have been limited. Silencing and the imposition of restrictions on the work professionals are allowed to do are key factors which can threaten any movement on the continuum. These measures can be used by employers to defend their own interests in response to wider pressures from the media, parents' pressure groups and public figures. Unlike some countries such as Scandinavia and the USA, freedom of speech is not guaranteed in British law. Most employees, particularly in local government, are subject to conditions of employment which restrict this right. This increases professional vulnerability to attack since their inability to share their situation isolates them from other members of the community.

As detailed in Chapter 7, supportive community groups can also be attacked but are not so easily controlled by other interests. Professional advocates therefore need to forge alliances with enlightened sections of the community and with survivors. The object is to maintain some room for manoeuvre against the pressures likely to 'close down' the advocate's activity, which would ensure a speedy return to the status quo. A public crisis of disbelief took place in Holland at the same time as events in Cleveland in response to the systematic abuse of a number of children in one community. Disbelief by the judicial authorities coupled with allegations in the press, focused the debate on what was alleged to be the phenomenon of mass hysteria rather than child abuse. The furore 'did not provoke further action . . . the attitude of the local government was to get back to normal as quickly as possible' (Jonke 1991). Summit (1988 pp.42–43) describes how similarly 'the active efforts of the public were directed towards containment, avoidance, and erasure' in the small community of Big Pine which 'sealed over without trace of it's scandal' following extensive abuse of children by a teacher known as 'Mr. Friendly'.

Advocates who are themselves abused professionally will probably have to live with persistent and prolonged lack of resolution of community conflicts whilst bearing the burden of knowing about abused children and colleagues who have been unjustly treated. This mirrors the dynamics of abuse. Unsurprisingly a professional 'accommodation syndrome' can easily ensue, in which reluctance to be pro-active on behalf of children leads to acceptance of an orthodoxy which best serves adult agendas. Fears that 'abuse by the system ' is as bad as if not worse than ongoing sexual abuse are exacerbated by lack of treatment facilities and lead to doubt about what being child-centred actually means. Individual professionals and agencies will resolve these conflicts in different ways. Their 'solutions' generate fresh problems which result from parties being at different points on the continuum. This reality is confirmed by the Cleveland report, (Butler-Sloss, 1988, p.82) which notes that Sue Richardson's 'commitment to the protection of children and recognition of the problems of child sexual abuse led her forward at a faster rate than the Police were prepared or able to go'. The conclusion is drawn that in her working context this gave her a 'significant share of responsibility for the breakdown in relationship between the two departments'. The report comments that in a different context, such as that of a children's rights organisation, there was much in her attitude and approach which would have been commendable', however,'the reality was that she occupied a position of some considerable importance and influence in a local authority', and any advice given should have been weighed 'not only with the interests of children but also . . . the good name of Cleveland Social Services and the wider public interest'. (Butler-Sloss 1988 pp.82–83). The message seems to be that the climate in which professionals can work should be dictated by those at the lower end of the continuum, and that unequivocal child advocacy potentially threatens wider interests. Such factors prevent workers uniting in defence of their own and children's interests. The private anguish is not voiced. Professionals are expected to remain detached from events and even from their own pain. It is as if the message has to be sanitised to be professionally accepted or understood. A distancing mechanism takes place, even from other beleaguered colleagues who fear adding to their own problems.

What can be done to prevent this isolation and silence? Miller (1983 and 1985) talks of the importance for victims of having an advocate who will stand by them unequivocally. Advocates themselves need help in the task of identifying with the suffering child, to cope with the impact of the child's pain on their own inner world. Additionally, the advocate who chooses not to act as a 'servile representative of society' (Miller, 1985 p.155) will encounter external pressures. Without advocacy for the advocate, which often means relying on peers, it can be difficult to sustain the risks inherent in adopting a child-centred position on the continuum. In the external world, trade unions, professional associations, community groups and civil rights campaigners can all assist in breaking the trap of silence. This would ensure support for professionals.

Conclusion: New Orthodoxy or New Dilemmas?

La Fontaine (1990) questions how far procedural responses can ever be adequate to the complex task of child protection. For example, Spicer (1990, p. 67) emphasises that the legal advice given to local authorities often leads to statutory duties being misunderstood:

> The correct question following investigation is 'Am I satisfied that the child will be safe?' A lack of information then leads to proceedings being taken. If the wrong question is asked, as it often is, namely 'Am I satisfied that the child will be abused?,' a lack of information regarding future risk will lead to no proceedings being taken.

This kind of flexible thinking is difficult for organisations which are built to maintain stability rather than promote change. This results in their being ill-equipped to respond to the challenge of the emergence of child sexual abuse (Richardson, 1989). Attempts to build an orthodoxy in the midst of rapid change are doomed to failure.

We emphasise throughout this book that the development of practice should be informed by a guiding ethos of child advocacy. Here we suggest three further 'landmarks in the fog'. First, there is the knowledge to be gained from listening to and believing adult survivors. Professionals should consider with Summit (1988, p.52) that 'even the distorted recollections of someone who has survived the journey might be more reliable than the beautiful engravings of landlocked geographers'. Second, we know that the energy inherent in the experience of trauma can be harnessed for healing and change, including social change. Survivors of other traumas, such as the holocaust and Vietnam, have shown that development of a 'survivor mission' is an important component in recovery. This can literally keep people alive and promote healing. Professionals should actively seek partnership with survivors to use the contribution many will wish to make from their experiences. To prevent empowerment becoming an empty slogan, Elias (1986, p.217) notes that 'designing measures for victim advocacy and protection must do more than create programs and remedial and legal structures - they must beckon victims to help liberate themselves'. In examining the historical decline in the power and status of victims of crime, Elias (1986, p.218) argues that 'perceived and temporary remedies' have been pursued for victims rather than 'policies, structures and systems that might prevent oppression in the first place'. An alliance of child advocates is potentially de-stabilising since it will militate against containment of the problem, which is numerically large, and threaten the stability of existing structures such as the family.

Our third landmark is the refusal to be 'cordoned off by signs full of prohibitions if the routes to new insights are to remain open in all directions' (Miller 1985, p.5). Post-Cleveland practice has appeared cordoned off by the process of giving adult rights more consideration than is given to other vulnerable groups. It is acceptable to argue for the option of authoritative intervention or greater legal safeguards in respect of physically abused children, the elderly, persons with learning difficulties and even bereaved children. Retaining this perspective in sexual abuse would allow greater flexibility in devising a tailor-made package for the child. Professional stuckness in a repetitive cycle of inaction may be more likely where practice is informed by key elements of the 'new orthodoxy'. These include reliance on procedural and administrative solutions which may be designed to limit cases to numbers with which existing resources can cope.

In our opinion the new orthodoxy means that in practice, only Group A children will be identified. By and large, children in Group B will be left to make their own way up the continuum. Since acting on behalf of Group B children may mean a decision to remove them from home, the disappearance of this group is consistent with a strong ethos of preventing family breakup. This may be accompanied by a move to treatment programmes for perpetrators, the efficacy of which is as yet unproven, at a time when treatment resources are not available for other family members. This diminishes the emphasis on the child's rights and the attempt to reconcile conflicting interests and philosophies seems likely to fail. There seems to be a strong consensus among adults that conflict should be avoided to prevent these issues from emerging. This consensus allows us to pretend that practice and legislation are working in the best interests of children. Rather than being community based, the process is kept within professional control, thus remaining divorced from its wider political and social context. There is no-one left to say 'The emperor has no clothes'.

We are uncertain whether we can or should try to establish an orthodoxy in a rapidly changing field of knowledge in which only perpetrators and their victims are truly informed. Our emphasis is on finding ways to maintain creativity and flexibility within a framework of child advocacy. The sheer scale of the problem, and the ever-approaching danger of 'exhaustion of the system' (Lynch, 1990) make it impossible to protect all the children who need it. Society must voice a new intention to care for children and thereby to break the cycle of damage for the adults of the future. In striving towards this ideal it must befaced that interim measures involve unpalatable choices in which some children may be sacrificed. For example, it may be most effective to devote the resources we do have to the youngest children where intervention and treatment pay the highest dividends in the long-term. As we learned in Cleveland, these children are the hardest to reach and help. We cannot however afford to reject those children, now adults, whose needs for early intervention were neglected. It is essential not to gloss over the unsatisfactory reality of such choices or to pretend they are solutions. To do so risks losing the vision of the 'caring society' which needs to be held at the forefront of our minds. One question which still requires an answer should be asked: what would society want and support professionals to do if all the children of Cleveland could have been definitely shown to have been abused ?

FIFTEEN MYTHS about

CHILD SEXUAL ABUSE and CLEVELAND

We are all concerned about child sexual abuse. But we haven't been told the truth ....

"Drs. Higgs and Wyatt screened all children for child sexual abuse whether or not there was any suggestion that it had taken place."

The Butler-Sloss Report emphasises that there was no screening. Only a tiny proportion of all the children seen by the paediatricians were examined for sexual abuse, and only if there was obvious good reason to think it might have happened. Many of the children had been sent to the General only because a parent, grandparent, teacher, doctor or health visitor was worried that the child was possibly being abused.

"Sexual abuse was diagnosed on the basis of just one sign – anal dilatation."

Anal dilatation was never the only reason for diagnosis, and in only a few cases was it the only physical sign. Doctors usually diagnose sexual abuse from a combination of physical signs and other evidence; for example, children with unusual sexual knowledge or behaviour, or children living with a man already convicted of buggery.

"Children taken to the General because of other problems, like constipation, were automatically suspected of being abused"

Some childhood problems such as constipation and "failure to thrive" can be due to sexual abuse and it would be negligent not to consider the possibility. No conditions went untreated, though sometimes the right treatment was to let the condition resolve by itself – constipation due to anal abuse gets better when the abuse is stopped.

"Examining children for sexual abuse is a form of abuse itself. It can hurt them and makes them prematurely sexually aware."

Children are only 'sexualised' if their sexual response is stimulated. An overall paediatric examination does not do this. It does not hurt because it is not internal; it consists of careful observation. Many children find it easier to tell of abuse after they have been examined; it is a natural way to begin gently asking the child about what has happened, and the child feels the examiner will believe him or her. Telling about the abuse often comes as a tremendous relief to the children. Children can be saved from years of abuse by early detection.

"Children were removed from their homes for the flimsiest reasons."

Children were admitted to hospital only on the strongest medical grounds - the need for further investigation in a safe and neutral environment. Most parents agreed to this, and they were invited to stay in hospital with the children. Where there was evidence that a baby or toddler too young to talk had been abused, a longer period away from home was sometimes necessary for investigation. In every case the intention was to resolve the problem, to ensure that the child could return home to a safe environment. This is not a flimsy reason.

Produced by CAUSE, a growing community initiative to prevent child sexual abuse. Tel 820950, 559327 or 813483

Continued

"All the 98 children now back at home were allowed home because the diagnosis was discredited."

Of course children are returned home as soon as possible, as long as their safety can be ensured. Some of the 98 are at home because the suspected abuser has left home or been arrested. Some are still wards of court, and some are still under the supervision of the social services department.

"Now that Dr Higgs + Dr Wyatt are not dealing with sexual abuse, the numbers of children diagnosed as sexually abused have fallen dramatically - or now the same as in other parts of the country?"

Wrong. As a result of the 'Cleveland crisis' the numbers of children reporting sexual abuse have risen greatly here and all over the country. Many social services departments are now facing their own 'crisis' as doctors and health visitors learn to recognise the signs of sexual abuse in children. But those children who need others to reveal the abuse (babies and toddlers too young to talk) are less well protected in Cleveland now. Often paediatricians diagnose sexual abuse but police surgeons, less experienced in recognising it, fail to confirm it.

"Abused children would always speak out about what is happening to them."

They rarely do. Children usually feel the abuse was somehow their fault; they feel guilty and ashamed. Most want the abuse to stop but are

threatened so they do not tell. E.g. 'If you tell, Mum will be very angry.' 'If you tell I will hurt you.'

"Sexual abuse doesn't do much harm."

Sexual abuse in childhood can do lasting damage; it leads to self-hatred, depression, inability to make or maintain relationships, sexual problems and suicidal tendencies. That's on top of the risk of physical damage and venereal diseases.

"Child sexual abusers are perverts; child sex abuse is very rare."

The evidence suggests that child abusers may appear perfectly normal men and women, in a very few cases? All they have in common is that they sexually abuse children. Children are sexually abused in all social classes, in all parts of the country, all over the world, not just in Cleveland. As more and more adults come forward and admit to having been sexually abused in childhood, we realise just what a widespread problem it is.

"People who are concerned about child sex abuse are part of an anti-family conspiracy."

Wrong. Normal loving families are the best places for children to grow up in. But the presence of an abuser makes the family a dangerous place for a child. The paediatrician's first commitment is always to the child.

"Ordinary fathers now can't cuddle their children without falling under suspicion."

Yes they can. There is a world of difference between cuddling one's children and penetrating their vaginas, mouth or anus with finger or penis. Grown-ups know when they are doing something for their own sexual gratification.

"All this fuss about child sexual abuse is a modern invention."

Sexual abuse of children has happened throughout the ages. The psychoanalyst Sigmund Freud found that many of his severely disturbed women patients revealed a history of sexual abuse in childhood - so many that at last he decided they must be making it up! We have been disbelieving sex abuse victims ever since.

"Child sexual abuse was not a problem in Cleveland before Dr Higgs arrived."

Concern about the sexual abuse of children has been growing over the last few years. Doctors were becoming more aware of it well before 1987. Cleveland social workers also received training in helping abused children.

"All the 11 doctors who wrote to support Dr Higgs are opening old wounds out of misbaken loyalty to a colleague."

The wounds were not healed, but festering. As long as children are sexually abused paediatricians must try to help them. Widespread support for 'Cleveland Against Child Abuse' (CAACA) shows that the problem cannot be swept under the carpet forever.

Abbreviations

ARC   Area Review Committee

DHSS   Department of Health and Social Security

GP   General Practitioner

JCAC   Joint Child Abuse Committee

JCC   Joint Consultative Committee

MP   Member of Parliament

NSPCC National Society for the Prevention of Cruelty to Children

UK   United Kingdom

Bibliography

Appleyard, J. 'The Paediatrician's Perspective', in Davie, R. and Smith, P. (Eds.) *Child Sexual Abuse: The Way Forward After Cleveland,* (London: National Children's Bureau, 1990).

Bacon, H. and Oo, M. *Disclosures in Sexual Abuse: Timing and Relationship to Clinical Findings,* (Unpublished paper, 1989).

Bagley, C.and King, T. *Child Sexual Abuse: The Search for Healing,* (London: Tavistock Routledge, 1990).

Baker, A. and Duncan, S. 'Assessing the Child's Therapeutic Needs', Unpublished Conference presentation: *Not One More Child,* (Reading University, September 18th–20th, 1989).

Bainham, A.C. 'The Children Act 1989: Welfare and Non-Interventionism', *Family Law, Vol.20 (1990) 143–145.*

Bass, E. and Thornton, R. *I Never Told Anyone: Writings By Women Survivors of Child Sexual Abuse,* (New York: Harper and Rowe, 1983)

A Child in Trust: The Report of the Panel of Inquiry into the Circumstances Surrounding the Death of Jasmine Beckford. (London: Borough of Brent, 1985).

Bentovim, A.'The Diagnosis of Child Sexual Abuse', in *Child Sexual Abuse in the Family and Related Papers,* (1987) 37–51 (Department of Psychological Medicine,Hospital for Sick Children,Great Ormond Street,London WC1 3JH).

Bentovim, A. Elton, A. Hildebrand, J. Tranter, M. and Vizard, E. (Eds.) *Child Sexual Abuse Within the Family:Assessment and Treatment,* (London: John Wright 1988).

Bolton, F. Morris L. and MacEachron, A. *Males at Risk: The Other Side of Child Sexual Abuse.* (London: Sage Books 1989).

Borge, T. Quoted in: Robinson W. and Norsworthy K. David and Goliath. (U.K: Zed Books) .

Briggs, S. (Professor of Theology,University of Southern California): personal communication, (1990).

Browne, A. and Finkelhor, D. 'Initial and Long-term Effects: A Review of the Research', in *A Sourcebook on child sexual abuse.* (London: Sage, 1986).

Brown, H. and Craft, A.(Eds.) *Thinking the Unthinkable: Papers on Sexual Abuse and People with Learning Difficulties,* (London: Family Planning Association, 1989).

Budin, E.L. and Johnson, C.F. 'Sex Abuse Prevention Programmes: Offenders' Attitudes about their Efficacy', in *Child Abuse and Neglect,* Vol.13. (1989) Number 1 pp77–87.

Butler-Sloss, Right Honorable Lord, E. *Report of the Inquiry into Child Abuse in Cleveland 1987,* (London: H M S O, 1988) .

Butler-Sloss, Right Honorable Lord,E. 'The Cleveland Inquiry', *Medico-Legal Journal* 57/3 (1989) pp149–163.

Butler-Sloss, Right Honorable Lord, E. 'Plenary Session' in Davie R. and Smith P.(Eds.) *Child Sexual Abuse: The Way Forward After Cleveland,* (London: National Children's Bureau, 1990).

Butler S. *Conspiracy of Silence: the Trauma of Incest,* (California: Volcano Press, 1985).

Campbell, B. *Unofficial secrets: Child Sexual Abuse: The Cleveland Case,* (London: Virago, 1988).

Cantwell, H. 'Update on Vaginal Inspection as it Relates to Child Sexual Abuse in Girls Under Thirteen', *Child Abuse and Neglect* 11 (1987) pp545–546.

Christiansen, J. and Blake, R. 'The Grooming Process in Father–Daughter Incest',in Horton,A. Johnson,B. Roundy,L and Williams,D.(Eds.) *The Incest Perpetrator: A Family Member No-One Wants To Treat.* (London: Sage, 1990).

Cleveland Child Protection Committee, *Annual Report* 1989/90. (Cleveland County Council, 1990)

Cleveland Rape Crisis Centre *Annual Report,* (1988) P.O.Box 31,Middlesbrough,Cleveland.

Coates, S. Clifford, L. Bacon, H. Gray, A. Jones, P. and Smith, J. 'Child Sexual Abuse: the Challenge to Clinical Psychology'. *Clinical Psychology Forum* No.30 December 1990: 11–15.

Report of the Committee of Inquiry into the Care and Supervision Provided in Relation to Maria Colwell, (London: H M S O, 1974).

Conerly, S. 'Assessment of Suspected Child Sexual Abuse', in Macfarlane, K. and Waterman, J.(Eds.) *Sexual Abuse of Young Children.* (London: Cassell, 1986).

Conte, J.R; Wolf, S; and Smith, T. 'What Sexual Offenders Tell Us About Prevention Strategies', *Child Abuse and Neglect,* Vol.13 (1989) Number 2, 293–301

Corwin,D.L.' Early Diagnosis of Child Sexual Abuse: Diminishing the Lasting Effects', in Wyatt G.E.and Powell G.J.(Eds.) *Lasting Effects of Child Sexual Abuse* (London: Sage, 1988).

Dawson, J.and Johnston, C. 'When The Truth Hurts'. *Community Care* 30th March (1989):pp 11–13

Dawson, J. 'Vortex of Evil'.*New Statesman,* 5 October (1990): pp12–14.

De Bono,E. *Conflicts: A Better Way to Resolve Them,* (Harmsworth: Penguin, 1985).

Department of Health, *Protecting children: A Guide for Social Workers Undertaking a Comprehensive Assessment,* (London:H M S O 1988)

Department of Health and Social Security *Child Abuse: Working Together: A Draft Guide For Inter-Agency Co-operation For the Protection of Children,* (London: H M S O, 1986)

Department of Health and Social Security, *Diagnosis of Child Sexual Abuse: Guidance For Doctors,* (London: H M S O, 1988).

Doyle,C. *Working With Abused Children,* (London: BASW Macmillan, 1990).

Driver, E. 'Through the Looking Glass', in *Child Sexual Abuse After Cleveland:Alternative strategies,* (London: Family Rights Group, 1988).

Driver, E. and Droisen,A. (Eds.) *Child Sexual Abuse: Feminist Perspectives,* (London: Macmillan, 1989).

Elias, R. *The Politics of Victimisation:Victims,Victimology and Human Rights,* (Oxford University Press, 1986).

Evans, C.M. and Walker-Smith, J.A. Correspondence.Management of Sexual Abuse, *Archives of Disease in Childhood* No.63 (1989): 678–679.

Ewbank, J.(1987) Re G (Minors) Child Abuse Evidence, Family Division,14 July 1986, in Stevens R.and Walsh (1987) (Eds.) *Family Law Reports Special Issue Number 4,*(1987) pp310–320.

Ferenczi, S. 'Confusion of Tongues Between Adults and the Child' (1932) in Masson J.M. *Freud:The assault on truth,* Appendix C, (London: Faber, 1984).

Ferguson, H. 'The Context of Cleveland: Global and Historical Perspectives', *Conference presentation, Newcastle upon – Tyne.* From Ferguson, H. and Ennew, J.,Social and Political Sciences Department, University of Cambridge, (1989).

Ferguson, H. 'Cleveland 1898: Has anything changes in 90 years?' *The Guardian* 3 May 1989, B.

Ferguson, H. 'Re-thinking Child Protection Practices: a Case for History', in *Taking Child Abuse Seriously: Contemporary Issues in Child Protection Theory and Practice,* Violence Against Children Study Group, (London: Unwin Hyman, 1990).

Finkelhor, D. Gomez-Swartz, B. and Horowitz, J. 'Professionals Responses', in Finkelhor, D. *Child Sexual Abuse: New Theory and Research,* (London: Collier Macmillan, 1984).

Finkelhor, D. *A Sourcebook on Child Sexual Abuse,* (London: Sage, 1986).

Finkelhor, D. 'Designing New Studies', in *A Sourcebook on Child Sexual Abuse,* (London: Sage, 1986).

Finkelhor D. 'The Trauma Of Sexual Abuse: Two Models', in: Wyatt, G.and Powell, G.J.(Eds.) *Lasting Effects of Child Sexual Abuse,* (London: Sage, 1988).

Flin, R. and Boon, J. 'The Child Witness in Court', in Wattam, C., Hughes, J. and Blagg, H. (Eds.) *Child Sexual Abuse,* (London: Longman, 1989).

Forfar, J.(Ed.) *The British Paediatric Association: Child Health in a Changing Society,* (Oxford University Press, 1988).

Fraser, S. *In My Fathers House: A Memoir of Incest and Healing.* (London: Virago, 1989).

Friedrich, W.N. 'Behaviour Problems in Sexually Abused Children: an Adaptational Approach', in Wyatt, G.E. and Johnson Powell, G.J. (Eds). *Lasting Effects of Child Sexual Abuse,* (London: Sage, 1988).

Freud, S. 'The Aetiology of hysteria', in J.M. Masson, *The Assault on Truth:Freuds Suppression of the Seduction Theory ,* Appendix B, (New York: Penguin, 1896).

Gale, J. 'Sexual Abuse in Young Children its Clinical Presentation and Characteristic Patterns', *Child Abuse and Neglect,* Vol.12 (1988) pp163–170.

Glaser, D.and Frosch, S. *Child Sexual Abuse*, (London: BASW/ Macmillan, 1989).

Gaulter, H. *The Origins and Progress of the Malignant Cholera in Manchester*, 1833)

Giarretto, H. *Integrated Treatment of Child Sexual Abuse: A Treatment and Training Manual*, (Palo Alto,California: Science and Behaviour Books, 1982).

Hallett, C. 'Child-Abuse Inquiries and Public Policy' in Stevenson,O (Ed.) *Child Abuse Public Policy and Professional Practice*, (London: Harvester Wheatsheaf, 1989).

Harrop, M. 'Public Silence – Personal Grief', *Child Abuse Review* Volume 4 (1990), Number 2 pp11.

Hawkins, P. and Shohet, R. *Supervision in the Helping Professions,* (Milton Keynes: Open University Press, 1989).

Hayter, T. *The Creation of World Poverty: An Alternative View to the Brandt Report*, (London: Pluto Press, 1981).

Henry, Whose Child? The Report of the Panel Appointed to Inquire Into the Death of Tyra Henry, (London: Borough of Lambeth, 1987).

H M S O, *An Introduction to the Children Act* (London, 1990).

Hill, M. The Manifest and Latent Lessons of Child Abuse Inquiries, *Br. Journal Social Work* 20 (1990) pp197–213.

Hindmann, J. *Step by Step :Sixteen Steps Towards Legally Sound Sexual Abuse Investigations*, (Oregon: Alexandra's Associates, 1987).

Hobbs, C.J.and Wynne, J.M. 'Buggery in Childhood – A Common Syndrome of Child Abuse'. *The Lancet*, 2 (1986) pp792–796.

Hobbs, C.J. and Wynne, J.M. 'Child Sexual Abuse – An Increasing Rate of Diagnosis', *The Lancet*. Oct.10 (1987) pp837–841.

Illesley, P. *The Drama of Cleveland,* (London: Campaign For Press and Broadcasting Freedom, 1990).

International Collaborative Committee For Child Health *The Medical Aspects of Child Abuse, Report of the Children's Research Fund*, 6 Castle Street, Liverpool L2 ONA, (1988).

Hopkins, J. 'Moving in a World of Shadows', *Social Work Today*, Vol 21, (1989)No.9: 17.

Jaudes, P.K.and Morris, M. 'Child Sexual Abuse: Who Goes Home?' *Child Abuse and Neglect* Vol.14 (1990) No.1 pp61–68

Jones, D.and McQuiston, M. *Interviewing the Sexually Abused Child,* (London: Royal College of Psychiatrists, Gaskell, 1988).

Johnson, T.C. 'Child Perpetrators: Children Who Molest Other Children: Preliminary Findings', *Child Abuse and Neglect,*Vol.12: 219–229.

Jonker, F. and Jonker-Bakker, P. 'Experiences with ritualistic child sexual abuse: a case study from the Netherlands', *Child Abuse and Neglect*, (1991), Vol.15, pp191–196

Kelly, R.J.and McCurry Scott, M., 'Sociocultural Considerations in Child Sexual Abuse', in MacFarlane,K.et.al .*Sexual Abuse of Young Children,* (USA: Guilford Press, 1986).

Kempe, C.H. 'Sexual Abuse, Another Hidden Paediatric Problem', *Paediatrics* 62 (1978) pp382–389.

Kempe, R.S. and Kempe,C.H. *Child Abuse*, (London: Fontana, Open Books, (1978).

Kennedy, M. 'The Abuse of Deaf Children', *Child Abuse Review*, Vol.3, (1989) pp3–7.

Kennedy, M. 'The Deaf Child Who is Sexually Abused – is there a Need For a Dual Specialist',*Child Abuse Review,*Vol.4, (1990) No.2 pp3–6.

Kennedy, R. 'Psychotherapy, Child Abuse and the Law', *Psychiatric Bulletin,13* (1989) pp471–476..

Kerns,D.L. 'Cool Science For a Hot Topic', *Child Abuse and Neglect* Vol.13 (1989) pp177–178.

Kidd, L. and Pringle,K. 'The Politics of Child Sexual Abuse', *Social Work Today*. 15th Sept.,Vol.20, (1988) No.3 pp14–15.

Kitzinger, J. 'Feminist Self-Help' in Rogers, W.F.,Hevey, D. and Ash, E,. *Child Abuse and Neglect, Facing the Challenge,* (London: Batsford, 1989).

Krugman, R.D. 'The more we learn the less we know with reasonable medical certainty?' *Child Abuse and Neglect* Vol.13 (1989) No.2 pp165–166.

La Fontaine,J. *Child Sexual Abuse*, (London: Polity Press, 1990).

Lestor, J. *Giving Children A Voice,* (London: Labour Party, 1990).

Leventhal, J. Bentovim, A. Elton, A. Tranter, M. and Reed, L. 'What to Ask When Sexual Abuse is Suspected', *Archives of Disease in Childhood.*Vol 62.(1987) Number 11 pp1188–1193.

Levy, A.(Editor), *Focus on Child Abuse – Medical, Legal and Social Work Perspectives*, (London: Hawkesmere, 1989).

Lindblad, F.'Child Sexual Abuse. The Suspects, the Suspicions and the Background', *Acta Paediatrica Scan.*79 (1990) pp98–106.

Long, S. 'Guidelines for Treating Young Children', in Macfarlane K.

and Waterman J. (Eds.) *Sexual Abuse of Young Children.Evaluation and Treatment,* (London: Cassesll, 1986).

Lynch, M. 'Ten Years of BASPCAN' *Child Abuse Review.* Vol.4. (1990) No.1.p.3.

MacFarlane K.and Waterman J.(Eds.) *Sexual Abuse of Young Children.Evaluation and Treatment,* (London: Cassell, (1986).

MacFarlane K. and Krebs S. 'Techniques for Interviewing and Evidence Gathering' in MacFarlane K. and Waterman J.(Eds.) *Sexual Abuse of Young Children.Evaluation and Treatment,* (London: Cassell,1986).

MacFarlane K. *Intervening in Child Sexual Abuse, Conference Proceedings,* Volume I.(1988) University of Glasgow Social Paediatric and Obstetric Research Unit and Department of Social Administration and Social Work.

Madara,E. 'Supporting Self-Help: A Clearing House Perspective', in *Social Policy* Fall (1987) p29.

Magnay,A.R.and Insley,J.'Anal Dilatation and Anal Dilatation Reflex Associated with Severe Haemorragic Colitis',(Letter) *Archives Disease in Childhood* 63 (1988) p679.

Meadow,R. 'Staying Cool on Child Abuse',. *British Medical Journal* (1987) pp295–345.

Menzie, I.L. *Containing Anxiety in Institutions: Selected Essays,* (London: Free Association Books, 1988).

Miller, A. *For Your Own Good: Hidden Cruelty in Childrearing and the Roots of Violence,* (London: Virago, 1983).

Miller, A. *Thou Shalt Not Be Aware: Societies Betrayal of the Child.,* (London: Pluto Press, 1985).

Miller, A. *Pictures of a Childhood,* (New York: Farrar,Straus and Giroux, 1986).

Miller, A. *The Drama of Being a Child,* (London: Virago, 1987).

Milne, A.A. *When We Were Very Young,* (London: Methuen, 1924).

Muram, D.'Child Sexual Abuse: Relationship Between Sexual Acts and Genital Findings', *Child Abuse and Neglect* Vol.13 (1989) pp211–216.

NSPCC. *Child Abuse in 1989,* Research Briefing No.11, (1990).

Nelson, J and Long,M. 'Trapped in the system: the experience of a team', *Child Abuse Review* Vol.2. (1988) No.2 pp10–11.

Newell, P. Children's Rights After Cleveland, in Riches, P. (ed.) *Responses to Cleveland: Improving Services for Child Sexual Abuse,* National Children's Bureau, (London: Whiting and Birch, 1989).

Nightingale, C. *Journey of a Survivor*, (Bristol,P.O.Box 529, 1988).

Ounsted, C. and Lynch, M. Family Pathology as seen in England.in Helfer, R. A. and Kempe, C.H. (Eds.) *Child Abuse and Neglect: The family and the Community*, (Massachusetts: Ballinger, 1976).

Pigot, His Honour Judge,T., Q.C. *Report of the Advisory Group on Video Evidence*, (London: Home Office, 1989).

Porter, R. (Ed.) *Child Sexual Abuse Within the Family*. Ciba Foundation, (London: Tavistock, 1984).

Powell, G.J. 'Child Sexual Abuse Research: the Implications for Clinical Practice, in Wyatt, G.E.and Powell, G.J.(Eds) *Lasting effects of Child Sexual Abuse* (London: Sage,1988).

Richardson, S. 'Child Sexual Abuse: The Challenge for the Organisation', in: Carter, P. Jeffs,T. and Smith, M.(Eds.) *Social Work and Social Welfare Yearbook I* . (Milton Keynes: Open University Press, 1988).

Richardson, S. and Bacon, H. 'Being There', in *The Cleveland Crisis, Five Perspectives. Association for Family Therapy Newsletter*, Vol.8. (1988) No.4 PP21–28.

Richardson. S. 'The Practitioner's View', *Community Care*, 11th July (1989) pp29–30.

Reinhart, M.A. 'Sexually Abused Boys', *Child Abuse and Neglect* 11 (1987) pp29–35.

Roberts, R.E.I. 'Examination of the Anus in Suspected Child Sexual Abuse', *The Lancet* November 8 (1986) pp1100.

Roundy, L.M. and Horton, A.L. 'Professional and Treatment Issues for Clinicians Who Intervene with Incest Perpetrators', in Horton, A; Johnson, B; Roundy, L; and Williams, D.(Eds.) *The Incest Perpetrator. A Family Member No-one Wants To Treat.* (London: Sage, 1990).

Rush, F. *The Best Kept Secret: Sexual Abuse of Children*, (Eaglewood Cliffs: Prentice Hall, 1980).

Russell,D.E.H. Schurman, R.A. and Trocki, K. 'The Long Term Effects of Incestuous Abuse: A Comparison of Afro-American and White American Victims', in Wyatt, G.E. and Powell, G .J.(Eds) *Lasting effects of child sexual abuse* (London: Sage, 1988).

Sgroi, S. *Handbook of Clinical Intervention in Child Sexual Abuse,* (Cambridge: Lexington Books, 1984).

Sharratt, J. 'Fleeting Glimpses of a Childhood and What it Means to 'let go' of Security', in *Journal of the Institute for Self-Analysis*, Volume 2, 1988, Number 1 P73

Sloan, J. and Murdoch,J. ' Professional Misconduct',in *Protecting Children into the 1990's: A Conference for Directors of Social Services and Child Protection Co-ordinators in the North of England* , North Yorkshire Social Services/Social Services Inspectorate (1990), pp26–27.

Smith, S. Forensic Medicine, (London: Churchill, 1945).

Social Services Inspectorate, *Report of an Inspection of Collaborative Working Arrangements Between Child Protection Agencies in Cleveland,* (Gateshead: Department of Health, 1990).

Southgate, J. 'The Hidden Child Within Us', in Rogers, W.S. Heney, D. and Ash, E.(Eds.) *Child Abuse and Neglect: Facing the Challenge,* (Milton Keynes: Open University Press,1989).

Spencer, M.J.and Dunklee, P. 'Sexual Abuse of Boys', *Paediatrics* 78 (1986) pp133–8.

Spicer, D 'The Lawyer's Perspective', in Davie, R. and Smith, P. (Eds) *Child Sexual Abuse: The Way Forward After Cleveland,* (London: National Children's Bureau, 1990).

Stephenson, O. (Ed.) *Child Abuse: Public Policy and Professional Practice,* (London: Harvester Wheatsheaf, 1989).

Stone, L.E. Tyler, R.P. and James, J.'Law Enforcement Officers as Investigators and Therapists in Child Sexual Abuse: A Training Model', *Child Abuse and Neglect* 8 (1984) pp75–82.

Stubbs, P. 'Developing Anti-Racist Practice: Problems and Possibilities',in Wattam, C. Hughes, J. and Blagg, H.(Eds.) *Child Sexual Abuse: Listening, Hearing and Validating the Experiences of Children,* (Harlow,Essex: Longman, 1989).

Summit, R.C. 'The Child Sexual Abuse Accommodation Syndrome', *Child Abuse and Neglect* 7 (1983) pp177–93.

Summit, R.C. 'Hidden Victims,Hidden Pain:Societal Avoidance of Child Sexual Abuse',in Wyatt, G.E.and Johnson Powell, G.J.(Eds). *Lasting Effects of Child Sexual Abuse* , (London: Sage, 1988).

Taylor, A.S. *A Manual of Medical Jurisprudence.* (London: Churchill, 1891).

Taubman, S. 'Incest in Context', *Social Work,* 29 (1984) pp35–40.

Tiernay, K.and Corwin, D. 'Exploring Intrafamilial Child Sexual Abuse.A Systems Approach',in Finkelhor D; Gelles R.J; Hotaling G.T.and Srauss M.A.(Eds.) *The Dark Side of Families,* (London :Sage, 1983).

Unicef Information Sheet No.8, (1988), 3/88,U.K.

United Nations Convention. *The Rights of the Child*. A/Res/44/25.5th Dec, (1989).

Vander Mey, B.J. 'The Sexual Victimisation of Male Children: A Review of Previous Research', *Child Abuse and Neglect,*Vol.12 , (1988) pp61–72.

Viinikka, S. 'Child Sexual Abuse and the Law' in Driver,E. and Droisen,A.(Eds.) *Child Sexual Abuse: Feminist Perspectives,* (London: Macmillan, 1989).

Vizard, E. Bentovim, A. and Tranter, M .'Interviewing Sexually Abused Children'. *Adoption and Fostering* Volume 11. (1987) No.1 pp20–25.

Waite, J Re.W (Minors) Child abuse: evidence,Re. in Stevens,R and Walsh,E.(Eds.) *Family Law Reports* Number 1 (1986) p280.

Wattam, C. Hughes, J. and Blagg, H. *NSPCC Child Sexual Abuse, Listening Hearing and Validating the Experiences of Children,* (Harlow: Longman, 1989).

Wattam, C. 'Investigating Child Sexual Abuse-a Question of Relevance'in Wattam, C. Hughes, J. and Blagg, H. *NSPCC Child Sexual Abuse,Listening Hearing and Validating the Experiences of Children,* (Harlow: Longman, 1989) p41.

Wells J.'Powerplays – Considerations in Communicating with Children'. in Wattam, C. Hughes, J.and Blagg, H. *NSPCC Child Sexual Abuse. Listening, Hearing, and Validating the Experiences of Children* (Harlow: Longman, 1989).

Westcott, H. Clifford, B. and Davies, G. *'Video Technology and Child Witnesses',* Paper presented to the British Psychological Society Annual Conference,4–8 April, 1990, Swansea,Wales.

Winnicott, D.W. 'Ego distortion in terms of true and false self', in Winnicott, D.W. *The Maturational Processes and the Facilitating Environment.*The International Psychoanalytical Library,No.64. London: Hogarth Press.

World Health Organisation *Targets for Health for All,2000 Implications for Nursing and Midwifery.,* (1986)

Wyatt, G.E. and Powell, G.J. (Eds.) *The Lasting Effects of Child Sexual Abuse,* (London: Sage, (1986).

Wynne, J.M. The Cleveland Report, *Child Abuse Review* Volume 2, (1988)Number 3 PP13–15.

Index

Accommodation, 77, 80, 100, 102
  syndrome, 72, 79
Adolescents who disclose, 84–85, 87–90, 95
Adult survivors of childhood sexual abuse,
  alliance with, 150
  empowerment of, 150
  as indicator of prevalence of c.s.a., 121
  insights from, 6, 10, 47, 78, 149–150
  recall of past abuse, 8, 78–79
  role in confronting societal denial, 63
  societal role of, 28, 124, 135
  support for, 50
Advisory Group on Video Evidence, Report
  of,
  see Pigot
Advocacy,
  for the child 18–19, 20–21, 32, 61, 73,
    75, 81, 107, 115, 136, 149, 150
  for the mother, 143
  responsibility of adults for, 19, 20, 61, 67,
    83
  for the professional, 145–149
Advocates,
  paediatricians as, 21, 47, 95
  role of, 21, 25, 32, 77, 81, 115–118, 137,
    139, 145, 148
Area Review Committee, 6–7, 10, 12

Baker and Duncan, a developmental model,
  84, 91
Beckford, Jasmine
  inquiry into the death of, 9
British Paediatric Association, 34
Butler,
  Sloss inquiry report,
    brief of, 31, 48–49

Sloss inquiry report, *cont.*
  interdisciplinary co-operation, 5, 11, 58
  interviewing of children, 107–108
  medical diagnosis, 45, 48, 49
  media, 101
  mothers, 101
  official solicitor, 32
  parents, 55
  perpetrators, 141
  police response, 13, 37
  referral rates, 11
Case conferences,
  diagnostic, 9
  parental participation in, 9–10
Case management, dilemmas of, 136
CAUSE, Cleveland against child abuse,
  alliance with professionals, 128–129
  formation of, 125
  opinion survey, 130
Children,
  Group A, 33, 38, *40–45,* 52, 55, 150
  Group B, 20, 33, 34, 38, *40–45,* 52, 55,
    59–60, 63, 150
  non-abused, 114
  placement following medical diagnosis,
    53, 73, 95, 99, 100
  position on continuum of disclosure, 72–
    74, 82–83, 94–95, 113
  pre-verbal, 66, 74, 100, 118
  rights, 17, 19, 131, 150
  who choose to leave family, 86–87, 93
  who disclose abuse once protected, 71–
    75, 81, 118
  who initiate investigation by disclosure,
    71–75, 81
  who molest other children, 79

165

About the Authors

Editors

SUE RICHARDSON, BA, Dip.App.SS, is a qualified social worker, family therapist and psychotherapist with extensive experience of work with children and families. As Child Abuse Consultant to Cleveland Social Services Department, she was a key figure in events leading to the Butler-Sloss Inquiry. She sees herself as an advocate for abused children, adults and their helpers and practices as an independent therapist, trainer and consultant. She is committed to sharing her experiences so others might feel empowered to act as child advocates.

HEATHER BACON, MA Child Development, is a Consultant Clinical Psychologist, trained in family therapy and specialising in work with children and families. She worked in Cleveland throughout the crisis. She has an enduring commitment to child advocacy and to finding ways for professionals from different disciplines to work together for the protection of abused children.

Contributors

MARJORIE DUNN, RGN, RHV, has considerable experience as a health visitor and was in the post of Nursing Officer at the time of the 'Cleveland Crisis'. She gave evidence to the Butler–Sloss Inquiry, has presented papers on her work at national and international level and has a particular interest in preventative work with families.

GEOFFREY WYATT, MBBS, MRCP, is a Consultant Paediatrician in Cleveland. His continuing commitment to pioneering child health in the urban community expanded to include child sexual abuse during events leading to the Butler-Sloss Inquiry in which he was a key figure.

MARIETTA HIGGS, MBBS, MRCP, is a Consultant Paediatrician in the North East of England. She is a graduate of the University of Adelaide Medical School and has worked in the UK since 1977. She was based in Cleveland during the events which led to the Butler-Sloss Inquiry. Dr Higgs places her commitment to the needs and rights of abused children in the context of her overall commitment to child health.

HILARY CASHMAN and ANNETTE LAMBALLE-ARMSTRONG are founder members of Cleveland Against Child Abuse, a unique community initiative. Annette has experience as a teacher, social worker and community educator. Hilary is a librarian and a member of the Community Health Council in Cleveland. Both are committed to bringing a lay perspective to bear on professional practice and ensuring the voice of the community is heard by decision makers.

WORK WITH PRISONERS

Brian Williams

Work with Prisoners is an authoritative guide for anyone working with people in prison. Using prisoners' own words, it describes how it feels to be in prison and what happens to people whilst they are inside. **FOR THE FIRST TIME** in one volume, this book brings together information about the responsibilities of the various caring professions in working with prisoners and the roles of others such as chaplains, psychologists and uniformed staff. It points the reader to other sources of information including prisoners' self-help groups.

Brian Williams is a lecturer in Social Work at the University of Sheffield. He was awarded the First Annual Prison Reform Trust Research Prize for research which contributed to this book.

Available September 1991
Price £8.45 (incl. 50p p&p)   *ISBN 0 900 102 799*

Available from Venture Press
Also in major bookshops   **Please see over for order form**

INTERPRETERS IN PUBLIC SERVICES

Phil Baker
with
Zahida Hussain and Jane Saunders

THE FIRST PRACTICAL GUIDE for policy makers and managers providing public services to a multi-lingual community, INTERPRETERS IN PUBLIC SERVICES is illustrated with many examples of how different public bodies are tackling the need for interpreting. IT

— includes Codes of Practice, sample record formats and discussion of the pros and cons of different forms of provision.

— draws together data from a wide variety of national and local sources to paint a compelling picture of continuing linguistic deprivation in Britain.

— makes the legal case for an implied duty to communicate which is being accepted by increasing numbers of public bodies.

— includes a chapter on practice in Community Relations Councils based on a unique survey which explores the potential contradictions between the Community Relations Councils' roles as service provider and as pressure group.

— gives a comprehensive review of the latest training possibilities for both community language interpreters and for those using their services.

— identifies gaps in social policy and administration courses, and post-qualification training, and suggests training approaches.

— identifies the next steps required in a process which is fast gaining its own momentum - the integration of interpreting provision as a basic element of services in multi-lingual areas.

Phil Baker is Head of Staff Development, Harlow Council. Zahida Hussain and Jane Saunders are trainers and consultants in equal opportunities.

Price £9.15 (incl. 50p p&p)   *ISBN 0 900102 79 9*

Available from Venture Press
Also in major bookshops   **See end of this book for order form**

HOME AND AWAY
Respite Care in the Community

Carol Robinson

ESSENTIAL READING for health and social services professionals, carers and families.

Family-based respite care is now recognised as a vital element of community care provision.

Dr Carol Robinson has written the first practical handbook for professionals, carers and families. Comprehensive and authoritative, it gives step-by-step advice on all aspects of establishing and running a respite care scheme, ranging from guidance on securing finance to more complex issues which may arise.

This highly readable guide sets respite care provision in its context by reflecting on the economic, social and legal perspectives. The result is an invaluable resource book.

The author is a Research Fellow at the Norah Fry Research Centre, University of Bristol. She has conducted extensive research into respite care and is currently working on a respite care project for young people with learning difficulties, funded by the Department of Health.

Price £8.45 (incl. 50p p&p)   *ISBN 0 900102 810*

Available from Venture Press
Also in major bookshops   **See end of this book for order form**

SEARCH
The Social Services consultancy and training
Directory 1991/2

— The FIRST directory of independent experts working in the social services and related fields, SEARCH offers national and regional information as a service to agencies across the disciplines.

— Entries from more than 300 consultants, trainers, independent social workers and researchers.

— Indexed by over 60 areas of work.

— ESSENTIAL READING for all local authority, health service and voluntary sector managers, lawyers and all who may need staff care, counselling and advice on social care issues.

Price £19.00 (incl. 50p p&p)   *ISBN 0 900102 82 9*

Available from Venture Press
Also in major bookshops   **See end of this book for order form**

ORDER FORM

If you wish to order any Venture Press title please complete the form below and return it to:
Venture Press, 16 Kent Street, Birmingham B5 6RD

Please send me _____ copies of _____

_____

I enclose a cheque payable to BASW Trading Ltd for £ _____

Name _____

Address _____

Please debit my Access/VISA Card no: (delete as appropriate) _____

Expiry Date _____

Please attach cardholder's name and address if different from above.

Signature _____ Date _____
(Negotiable rates for bulk orders)